Best
Wishes

Lisa Brown

Kyle

Katie

Kimberly

A Mother's
JOURNEY

Through Faith, Hope, and Courage

LISA BRODEUR

authorHOUSE®

AuthorHouse™ LLC
1663 Liberty Drive
Bloomington, IN 47403
www.authorhouse.com
Phone: 1-800-839-8640

This book is a work of non-fiction. Unless otherwise noted, the author and the publisher
make no explicit guarantees as to the accuracy of the information contained in this book
and in some cases, names of people and places have been altered to protect their privacy.

Published by AuthorHouse 10/17/2013

ISBN: 978-1-4918-2406-1 (sc)
ISBN: 978-1-4918-2405-4 (hc)
ISBN: 978-1-4918-2404-7 (e)

Library of Congress Control Number: 2013917982

Any people depicted in stock imagery provided by Thinkstock are models,
and such images are being used for illustrative purposes only.
Certain stock imagery © Thinkstock.

This book is printed on acid-free paper.

Because of the dynamic nature of the Internet, any web addresses or links contained in
this book may have changed since publication and may no longer be valid. The views
expressed in this work are solely those of the author and do not necessarily reflect the
views of the publisher, and the publisher hereby disclaims any responsibility for them.

This book is dedicated to the best husband, father, and friend I have ever known: Michael Brodeur. I am so blessed to have shared my life with him and to have had his beautiful children. He taught me so much, and together we made a very happy marriage and home. He always told me I was tough, but I didn't realize how tough I was until the minute I lost him. He may not be with me in person, but he has guided me in many decisions I've had to make. Michael fills a huge space in my heart, and I feel his presence always. I will love and miss him until the day we meet again.

This book is dedicated to my son Kyle, whose determination, strength, and love have gotten us through so many roller coaster rides. I wouldn't wish on anyone the ups and downs we have gone through together as mother and son since the time he was born. Kyle is an inspiration. Each and every day, I am amazed that he is a happy young man who is not bitter, despite all his losses in life. Kyle, you are the best son I could ever ask for. I love you.

This book is also dedicated to my daughters, Kimberly and Katie. You two girls had to go through such a terrible loss at a very young age. Losing your daddy was traumatizing. Having your brother disabled, yet being there every step of the way without complaining at such a young age, shows just how amazing you are. As a family we stayed together and stayed strong for each other. Both of you girls are such a blessing. Your strength, confidence, and belief that things would be okay have gotten us through! I am so blessed to have you both in my life. I love you both so very much!

To all my family and friends who were with us through this long, difficult time: I thank you so very much for all your love and support. I never would have survived without all the love, time, and patience that were given to each of us—especially with my daughters, who had a tough time. Thank you for your understanding and patience when their lives were turned upside down and they acted out. To everyone who took the time to listen to me: thank you for that simple hug and shoulder to lean on when I needed it so badly. To all the people who prayed for our family, stayed with Kyle, and visited us: thank you so much. I am so blessed to have each and every one of you. I never would have survived if it hadn't been for you all!

To all the doctors, nurses, therapists, and other staff at U-Mass, Spaulding, Children's Hospital, and Mass Hospital School: you all became a family to Kyle and me. We spent a great deal of time in each hospital, and we were always treated so wonderfully. Kyle was and still is a challenge. Whether the situation involves surgery, therapy, or a diagnosis, he loves to be different. Thank you for your patience and for never giving up on him. Thank you all for helping us transition to each new place. Kyle and I were blessed by each of you. You are all amazing people, and I thank you for all you do!

I hope you will find reading my book inspirational. I hope you never give up on your own personal journey. I hope that my book will be in all schools, all drug awareness programs, and all brain injury programs. I hope it will show you what a victim goes through when someone makes bad choices with drugs and alcohol. My family and I have managed to stay positive and to never give up, no matter what. Always remember that if you have faith, hope, and courage, you will overcome any obstacle.

Table of Contents

Chapter 1

Feeling sick to my stomach, not knowing what was wrong, feeling nauseated and then vomiting, I wondered, *Could it be?* Filled with joy and a hope that it was real, I soon realized that it was. I was pregnant!

I felt excitement and fear of what was ahead, and all the little flutters grew stronger and turned into kicks that woke me up at night. How I loved to rub and hold my belly, as I never had before, forming a love like no other. Then the pain started and turned into long, hard, painful contractions; the waiting to be told that it was time to push; and the burst of energy after fifteen hours of labor.

Finally, out came a little face, a handsome little baby boy with tiny fingers and toes. Looking at mommy for the first time, he cried, wanting to be held close and to feel the warmth of my body. I heard his little cries of hunger, day and night, as he waited to be fed, loved, held, and nurtured, knowing that he was loved by his mommy and daddy.

His little hands grew, and then he was sucking his thumb, holding his bottle, clapping, sitting up, crawling, and getting into everything. Before I knew it, he was walking and starting to talk, saying "juice" at the refrigerator and wondering where daddy was.

As he got older, I heard his footsteps as he ran around, his cute little voice so soft and gentle, his little arms reaching around my neck and holding me tight as he gave me a kiss like no other. What a joy, this love of my life. How could I have been so lucky? He waited by the windowsill, waiting for daddy to come and crying because he never came. Headed to preschool, he feared separation from me, not knowing what to expect. Soon he realized that his mom would be back, and his fear diminished as he had fun and made friends.

With the toddler years at an end, he grew into a kind and softhearted youth, playing T-ball, soccer, and basketball, joining the Cub Scouts, developing great coordination for bike stunts and rollerblading, and trying any activity that presented itself. This child was full of life and adventure, full of excitement as he came home coated in mud after catching a bullfrog in the river across the way.

What a son I have, I thought. I felt blessed as he taught his young sisters to love nature and life. He was so innocent, and yet I realized that his life was also painful. He missed his father, not understanding why he wouldn't be in his life. He cried behind a dumpster, wondering what he had done that was so wrong. He knew the man who was raising him as his own loved him, and he felt blessed to have him, but he was still confused.

Youth progressed to the adolescent years. He still wondered why his life was this way, but he knew his mommy loved him and a man he called daddy. He loved his dad like no other—as a friend, playmate, and teacher—and they shared a special bond that could not be broken. He learned kung fu and hockey, along with his other sports, which kept us very busy, and he enjoyed his sisters and family and going to school. Growing into a fine young boy, he realized that Santa Claus was not real and that fantasy was only fantasy.

When he turned ten years old and went into fifth grade, Kyle walked to school with his friend. At times he cried, not wanting to leave me, afraid of separation. But he came home after school every day and soon realized that his new school was fun and his teacher was awesome.

Kyle enjoyed a day of shopping with his sisters, Daddy, and me. He was excited to get home and show off his new rollerblades to me. He got in the van, put on Daddy's CD, and sang Daddy's soft music. The van went around a corner, and suddenly there was a crash, a big bang—and Kyle was getting weaker and weaker, his heart getting slower by the second. He didn't know what was happening. How could this be? All he wanted was to try his rollerblades!

But now he was fighting for his life.

Chapter 2

Mike and I honeymooned in Cancun, Mexico. The ocean was so blue, and the Mexicans were very nice—and drove very fast. Families sold custom-made jewelry, blankets, dolls, and shirts, trying to raise money—and there was my husband, trying to bargain to get a good deal. That's my Mike, always trying to save money. We had a great time, lots of one-on-one time and lots of romance. It went by so fast. It was a new beginning for the three of us, as we were a family now.

Kyle asking Daddy or me, to take him to soccer, baseball, basketball, kung fu, hockey, or Cub Scouts. Depending on what season it was, he kept us busy. Kyle was a very athletic young boy who loved sports and had great balance and coordination. He liked school, but he didn't love it. He hated homework, as he would rather be outside, running, rollerblading, or riding his bike.

Mike and I decided we wanted kids as soon as we could, since Kyle was already five. I got pregnant during our first month of marriage, and we were very excited. Kyle was even more excited. I always felt very sick and vomited a lot, especially during the first and last trimester, but I still managed to gain a lot of weight. Every night, Mike and Kyle felt the baby kick. Kyle wanted a brother, but Mike said he didn't care about that because he had his son already. He had Kyle. Mike had been with Kyle since Kyle was a year and a half old, and he couldn't have loved him more.

When it was time for an ultrasound, we wanted to know the news, and it was confirmed that we were having a little girl. Mike was thrilled: a little daughter, Daddy's little girl. I wanted a daughter also, and I was excited to buy all the dresses and bows. My baby shower was very nice, and I received everything I needed for our little bundle. Mike wanted to name our baby Madison, but I said no. I wanted to name her Kimberly after one of my friends. I suggested we name her Kimberly Madison, and he said okay, that we would do whatever I wanted.

Mike and I both worked at United Lens. We loved our jobs and the people we worked with. UL was very special to us, as this was where we had met and fallen in love. Mike and I had decided that when we had children I would no longer work full-time, so I could concentrate on raising our children. When I went into labor at work, I didn't want to leave, as I knew it would be my last day. I wanted to finish the work on my desk before I left, and my coworkers and boss were worried. They called Mike to come and take me home, but I refused. I had to finish what I'd started. You could say that I was stubborn, but leaving and knowing I wasn't coming back was very difficult for me. Mike just wanted us to go home and get ready to go to the hospital.

I finally left United Lens and went home, but I refused to go to the hospital. I knew it would be a long labor, and I didn't want to be at the hospital too early. Instead, trying to waste time, I said I wanted to go out to eat at the Kahula. Off we went—Mike, Kyle, and I. Aunt Jean, our waitress, was a nervous wreck when she found out I was having contractions. I couldn't eat; I just wanted to pass time. Later that night, I decided to go to the hospital, knowing it would be a very long night. Mike was very attentive to me, giving me ice chips and massaging me. He was great until early morning when he fell asleep, and then I needed ice chips and he wouldn't wake up! I yelled his name and threw stuff at him to finally wake him up.

My daughter Kimberly was born later that morning. Mike was all dressed up in the hospital scrubs, laughing and saying, "It's a girl! Now I have a wedding to pay for!" He was so excited. He came over to me and said, "Good job, Lisa," and gave me a kiss. Kimberly was so cute with her little rolls of baby fat and her light-brown hair. She weighed eight pounds, five ounces. I just couldn't wait for Kyle to meet his little sister.

My mother brought Kyle to visit his little sister. He was so excited, he couldn't wait to hold her, and he did a great job. Kyle actually did better than Mike did, because Mike was so nervous. If the baby cried, Mike wanted to know if Kyle wanted to hold her. It was hilarious, watching a grown man be so nervous, so afraid that he would drop her that he would ask a five-year-old to help.

The next day we brought our little bundle of joy home, we were so happy and excited. Kim seemed to grow very fast, and we enjoyed her very much. She walked at nine months of age. Kyle taught her a lot and always played with her. She was a tough little girl. Every night, Mike gave her a bath and then played with the two children before bedtime.

The first year went by fast. We booked a family vacation to Disneyland. Kyle was six, a great age, and Kim was turning one. We had a great vacation, and the kids loved the Disney characters and the parade and light shows. The highlight of the trip was when we met Michael Jackson at a show. My Mike was so excited that he took Kyle and went to get Michael's autograph. I stayed seated and felt bad for Mike, as I wanted Mike to just let Michael Jackson enjoy the show, but Mike was very excited and even started videotaping. Mike and Kyle had a great night, and Kyle was grinning ear-to-ear as he held his autograph from Michael Jackson.

After breakfast on our last morning there, I started to feel sick. I told Mike that I was nauseated and felt like I was going to vomit. He said, "Oh boy!" I said excitedly, "I bet I'm pregnant." I wanted another little girl, and I wanted Kimberly to have a little sister. I would buy a pregnancy test as soon as we got home.

Mike was at his baseball game, when Kyle, Kimberly, and I went to go see him. With a big smile I said, "You're going to be a daddy!" He said, "Oh boy! Don't tell my mother until I am home." When Mike arrived home, his mother came over. He told her, "Lisa's pregnant!" Rita said, "Oh boy! You're going to be busy."

Kim had just turned one, but we wanted our children close together in age. Mike and I were both the youngest of eight children. Our birthdays were only one day apart in September, but there was a nine-year difference. It was great that we had siblings close in age, and I was glad that our children would be born close together also.

Mike and I got along great. If a decision had to be made, we did it together. He left the kid stuff up to me, and he took care of all the bills and problems. I had no worries, as he made my life stress-free. I just concerned myself with cooking, cleaning, shopping, and taking care of the kids. If the kids ever needed something, all I had to do was tell him, and off we went to get it. We never went without. We were very blessed in that way—and to have found each other.

Kyle loved his little sister Kimberly. He always spent a lot of time with her, comforting, feeding, tickling, and teasing her. By the time she was two years old she was a little tomboy. He even taught her how to jump out of her crib. Even though there was a five-and-a-half-year difference between them, he spent much quality time with her, and she loved her brother. When Kyle found out that we were going to have another baby in the house, he was happy, but I could see that he was also jealous.

This pregnancy just seemed to fly by. I was sick and vomiting a lot, and of course I gained a lot of weight again, but Mike never complained. He just said, "You're pregnant. You'll lose it afterward. Don't worry." Mike and the kids loved to rub my belly at night to see if the baby would kick or move. We found out that we were having another girl, and we were thrilled, as I'd wanted Kim to have a sister.

Katie was born on December 30, 1993. She was big, with so many little rolls, and she weighed eight pounds, twelve and a half ounces. This time it was a very fast labor. We were glad she arrived after Christmas and before the New Year, as Mike wanted the tax deduction. That's my Mike, always thinking.

Coming home with Katie was so nice. Now that we had three kids, I was very busy. I was nursing a newborn, Kim was only twenty months old, and Kyle was six years old. Kyle and Kim were very jealous, as the baby consumed much of my time. I included the older kids in Katie's care—bathing, changing diapers, dressing her, or just holding her. Especially while I was nursing, I would read Kim a book.

When Mike came home, he was a big help. He always handled bath time and played with the kids on the floor. We had to take Kyle to some activity every night, and of course we helped him with homework. We were a great team, getting everything done. Mike's mom loved to rock the girls and sing them nursery rhymes. She just loved them so much. Uncle Ronald, Aunt Gloria, and Aunt Jean came to visit at least once a day. It was so nice living next to family. I was never lonely, and a helping hand was always available if I needed one.

When Katie was one and a half years old and Kim three, I was asked to come back to work at United Lens, part-time. I was thrilled, but Mike wasn't. He didn't want me going back, as he thought I was busy enough. I wanted to, so I took the job—three hours a day, five days a week. It was perfect for me. Mike agreed but not happily, as he was worried about the kids. At first I had family sitting for us. Then, after a few months, I brought them to a sitter. The girls loved it, and the sitter Lori was incredible. It all worked out very well.

Our sixth wedding anniversary was coming, and I had saved enough money to surprise Mike with a trip to Las Vegas. I knew he had always wanted to go, but we'd never had the chance, especially having two little ones. On our anniversary, Mike took me out to eat, and I gave my gift to him then. I was in tears giving it to him, because I knew how happy he would be. He was in shock that I had saved enough money to pay for the trip. We took Kyle with us so he could visit his cousin that lived there. We had a wonderful time, and it's a memory I will never forget. It was a special anniversary, and I have spent the happiest years of my life with this beautiful man. I feel so blessed to have him.

Kyle was going through a stage of missing his biological father, not understanding why his father wasn't in his life. Over the years, he had come once in a while, but he was never consistent. There were times when Kyle waited by the windowsill for his father's truck to pull up, but he never showed up, and Kyle was heartbroken. Kyle wanted to know what he had done wrong. I explained to him that he had done nothing wrong. I never wanted to talk negatively about his father, so I would say, "He must be working a lot, and he must be busy."

As time went on, Kyle still couldn't accept the way things were. He loved Mike more than anything, but he knew that his biological father was around, and he couldn't see him. One day he said to me, "How come I am not a Brodeur? Kim, Katie, and you are. I want to be too!" I gave him a hug and explained that he had his biological father's name and that I was a Brodeur because I had married Daddy. I told him we were all the same. Kyle said tearfully, "I want to be a Brodeur." I said I would talk to his dad and ask him if he would allow us to add Brodeur to his name.

I went downstairs in tears. Mike was worried and asked me what was wrong. I told him that Kyle felt that he didn't belong to our family because his last name was Tremblay instead of Brodeur. Mike felt awful and said, "What do you think we should do?" I said, "Do you think maybe we can add Brodeur to his name?" He said, "I think Kyle's father has to give permission for that."

I hadn't spoken to Kyle's father in a year or so, but I decided to call him. I asked him if he would be willing to add Brodeur to Kyle's name, explaining what Kyle was going through. He said, "No way," but I couldn't understand why, because he wasn't even in Kyle's life. Then he hung up on me.

I was upset when I told Mike that the answer was no. "Now what do we do?" I asked.

Mike said, "Lisa, what if I adopt Kyle? He's my son anyway. Why not make it legal? That way I never have to worry about losing him if something were to happen to you."

I was in shock. "Really? Adopt him? You wouldn't mind?" I knew that was a lot of responsibility to take on.

He said, "No, I love him. Once Kyle's father realizes what adoption means hopefully he will agree to it."

I called Kyle's father back and said nervously, "I have something very important to ask you."

He said, "What? I'm not doing a name change!"

I said, "I know that. But would you allow Mike to adopt Kyle? Explaining to him what adoption would mean. You don't see him, and he needs that sense of belonging to grow up healthy."

I said, "You would be giving up all rights to him, and Mike would be his legal father."

He said, "Draw up the papers, and I'll sign them."

I said, "Okay, I'll be in touch." I hung up the phone in tears and ran into Mike's arms, happy but feeling hurt, and told Mike, "He said yes! You can adopt Kyle!"

With a big smile, Mike said, "Now I will never have to worry about losing my son. I love that little boy more than anything, I'm so proud that he will have my name."

We both went upstairs to tell Kyle, as he was in bed. Mike said, "Kyle, how would you feel about Daddy adopting you?"

Kyle asked, "What is *adopting*?"

Mike explained. "Adoption would mean that you are my child, legally, just like Kim and Katie. No one could ever take you away from me, even if something happened to your mother. The best part is that your name will be Kyle Brodeur!"

"Just like everyone else in the house! Really?" With a big smile, Kyle hugged us both tight, and Daddy told him how much he loved him and depended on him, especially in taking care of his sisters and his mom when he wasn't home. "You're the man of the house, kiddo," Mike said. "Good night. I love you!"

Mike wasted no time. He called an attorney first thing in the morning, and we went to our appointment later that week. We were very excited as the attorney drew up the papers and Kyle's father signed them. After returning the signed papers, we got a court date. Kyle was so happy to start school that September as a Brodeur.

That weekend it was Mike's and my birthdays. We always celebrated our birthdays together—his on September tenth and mine on the ninth. I was turning thirty and Mike was turning thirty-nine. Kyle had a soccer game that morning. After the game, we arrived home—and what a shock I had! Mike had managed to surprise me with a thirtieth birthday party. It was the only time I had ever been surprised in my life, and all my friends and family were there. It was so special. Mike's family had worked really hard at keeping the party a secret from me and hiding the food. Living next door to each other, it would have been easy to slip up, but they managed to hide everything from me.

Mike had thought of everything. He'd had the kids make me special plates. Kyle's plate displayed his famous dog picture, and the girl's—ages three and five—had colored with markers. The plates came out so nice. The next present he gave me was just unbelievable. He had made me a CD of him singing love songs. Mike had a beautiful voice, and only months earlier, the whole family had found out that he could sing, as he had never let anyone hear his voice. One day at a party, he had decided to sing, and after he was done, he'd received a standing ovation from two hundred people. It was beautiful! And now I had a CD that I could listen to whenever I wanted. What a treasure! He gave me such a wonderful memory and a beautiful day.

Kyle's adoption day had finally come. I was so happy for Kyle, knowing that he would legally be a Brodeur by that afternoon, knowing that if something ever happened to me, Kyle would stay with Mike. Kyle could never be taken away from his family. In the courtroom, Kyle looking so handsome in his dress pants and shirt, and Mike looked so happy. The judge asked Mike if he understood the responsibility that he was taking on. Mike said yes and looked at Kyle, smiling. The judge said to Kyle, "Your new name is Kyle David Brodeur, and the best of luck to all of you."

We left that courtroom so happy. It was legal now. Kyle had received his wish, and he was so excited to be a Brodeur! No more worries for any of us!

Chapter 3

It was a beautiful fall October day, and the trees were full of color. The kids were playing outside and waiting for their daddy to pull into the driveway. Their daddy had been gone for two weeks and was coming home from England.

Going to England had always been a dream for Michael. One day my father had come over, wanting to know if Mike would go to England with him to pick out some canaries. My father raised birds, and he would go anywhere to get the best birds. In shock, Mike asked, "All the way to England for birds?" This was what my father wanted, and an all-expense-paid trip to go to the place of Michael's dreams was too good to be true.

Mike kept telling me, "Why don't you go? It's your father. I will take care of the kids." I would have loved to go, but it was more important to me that he went. I wanted Mike to have fun and do something different. He deserved to go and do something for himself, and I knew he would be a great help to my father. With our children being so young and the cost of everything, it would have been impossible to go as a family. So I told him to go and have fun!

A few weeks before he was to leave, we went shopping at the mall. Mike picked out a blue spring jacket. He looked so handsome in it. I loved it! He needed sneakers, and Kyle picked those out because he knew his dad's taste. We called them "plain Jane sneakers," as Mike would only wear white shoes without any other color on them. This was always a big joke, and Kyle thought it was so funny. As Mike tried on the sneakers, the girls jumped on his back for a piggyback ride, and he kidded around, saying, "Lisa, help me!" Mike got down to their level on his knees and asked, "Girls, how can Daddy try on sneakers with you all over my back?" The girls laughed, as it was a game to them. I was no better. I laughed too. I just loved watching him play with the kids.

As we waited at home for Mike's return from his trip to England, I was in the kitchen, cooking him a ham dinner and thinking he would be happy to have a home-cooked meal when he arrived. I was so excited for his arrival. I had missed him very much, and I was tearful just thinking about his coming home. I wanted a hug so badly. Two nights earlier, I had dreamed that two people had died, waking up instantly. Maybe I was afraid of Mike flying so far overseas, thinking that something could go wrong with the plane. Just thinking of that dream scared me. I couldn't bear to lose my father and husband. I knew he should be home shortly, as he had a limo driver bringing him home.

As I watched for him through the window, a white car pulled up. I quickly went outside onto the porch. Mike got out, knelt down, and kissed the ground! I stood on the porch, wondering what he was doing, kissing the ground before he kissed me. He got up with his bag in hand, came over to me, and hugged me tight. He kissed me, told me he loved me, and said how much he'd missed me. I was in tears, relieved that he was home. He said he'd had a dream that he died. In shock, I told him about my dream. We both couldn't believe we'd had the same dream. We were so thankful that no one had died and he was home safe.

The kids were at the home of their grandmother, Meme Rita, when Mike arrived, and they were excited to come home and see Daddy—and his gifts for them from England. He'd brought home Beanie Babies, which the kids collected, T-shirts and other goodies. The girls wouldn't leave him alone, even sitting on his lap at the dinner table. They just wanted to play. Kyle sat in his chair with a big smile, telling Mike all about kung fu and his last two weeks in school. We had a great meal, and Mike loved his ham dinner. It was so nice having him back home.

The nights had been long without him. I told him I'd had trouble sleeping and that I couldn't wait to be in his arms again.

That night also happened to be Halloween, and it was getting dark outside. It was time for trick-or-treating, but I told Mike that if he was too tired to participate he could rest and unpack and I would take the kids. He wouldn't hear of that. He was going, not wanting to miss out. I had made Kimberly and Katie little witch costumes, and Kyle was dressed as an Army guy. The kids wanted Mike and me to dress up also, so I put on a witch costume I happened to have, and Mike put on his Army outfit. Kyle and Mike were like twins, their faces colored with green paint, and we girls were witches.

Off we went, trick-or-treating to people we knew. Everyone was excited to hear how Mike's trip had been. We went trick-or-treating to Albert DiGregorio house. Al was the owner of United Lens Company, and he took a nice family picture of us that night. His wife, Doris, always bought the kids something special. Al was eager to hear about Mike's trip, but the kids wanted to leave. The kids received lots of candy that night, especially from Uncle Ronald and Aunt Gloria, Meme, and their great-grandfather. We couldn't have asked for a better family night out. It was so nice, and everyone was so happy—especially to have Daddy back home.

After arriving home, we sorted through the candy. The kids were so happy. It had been a full day with much excitement, and now it was bedtime. Mike and I tucked the kids in, and Mike read them a bedtime story. After that story, the girls wanted more, but they wanted Daddy to make up his own story, so he did. Mike's stories were always about something the girls had done. It was a special time, and the girls always giggled.

Then it was Kyle's turn. Sometimes Kyle just wanted to talk about his sports or what was happening the next day. He was excited to have Daddy home, and I heard him say, "I love you, Daddy." And Mike said, "Thank you for helping your mom take care of the girls." Mike kissed Kyle good night and said, "Love you, kiddo. See you in the morning." I was thinking how lucky I was to have such a good man in my life and how much I loved him!

As I was sitting on the couch, Mike came to sit next to me. We cuddled, talking about his trip and our family night together. He thought that the girls had grown in the past two weeks. He said, "You know what I missed most while I was gone? Family time just being together like tonight." I hugged him and said that I was so glad he was safe at home. Starting to kiss, we went to bed and had a wonderful night.

Lisa and Mike in 1994.

Kyle as a child, 1989,
with his mother Lisa.

Kyle as a child in 1991, and his
father Michael on this wedding day.

Michael and his three children, Kyle, Kimberly, and Katie,
on their first day of school in September of 1997.

Kyle, 9 years old, with his sisters Kimberly and Katie, 1996.

Chapter 4

It was such a gloomy day. It was raining on and off with torrential downpours. To me it didn't matter what the weather was like, because Mike was home and my family was together. Mike had only been gone for two weeks, but I had missed him so much. Around lunchtime, Mike asked me if I wanted to go to the Auburn Mall and start Christmas shopping. Of course I said yes! He said some hockey players were at the mall, and he thought Kyle would like to get their autographs. I thought it was great idea.

While I was getting ready, the girls were with their daddy in the living room. Mike put on the Princess Diana song, "Candle in the Wind" by Elton John. It was a beautiful song, and since Mike had just come back from England, it meant even more to him and me. The song was playing, and Mike asked Katie and Kimberly if they wanted to dance with Daddy. Both girls jumped up to dance, but Katie wanted Daddy to herself, and Kimberly let her. Mike wanted to give Kimberly a chance to dance too, but Katie got upset whenever he tried. Mike got some time alone with Kimberly, and when Katie kept interrupting, he kept telling Kim that she was such a big girl to give in to Katie. I thought it was so beautiful that I got the video camera out. Kyle had been outside riding his bike. He came in while the girls were dancing with their father and asked excitedly if we were ready to go to the mall.

As we drove to the mall, it rained heavily at times. Kyle was excited to get autographs from hockey players, so he and Mike went there first. Kyle came running back to show me the signatures.

Our first shopping stop was a sports store. Kyle asked me if he could get some new Rollerblades. I didn't want to say no to him, so I told him to go ask his daddy. Christmas was only eight weeks away, so I figured I would let Mike handle it. Kyle went to his father, and I saw them looking at some Rollerblades. Kyle found some really nice ones for a hundred dollars. From a distance, Kyle looked at me with a big smile. I just knew Mike wouldn't be able to say no! Mike came to me and said, "What do you think?" I smiled and said, "It's fine with me!" Mike said, "Well, it's not like he wouldn't be using them. That's all Kyle does at home—rollerblade and ride his bike." We went to cash out, and Kyle was the happiest boy. He couldn't wait to test them out, but the weather was so bad that we told him he would have to wait for the next day. Even so, he was grinning from ear to ear!

The girls were hungry and asked to eat at Papa Gino's. They wanted pizza, everyone's favorite. We had a very nice supper, and everyone was happy to have Daddy with us. We talked a little about his trip. He'd had a wonderful time, and he kept telling me that he wanted to take me to England someday. The girls just wanted his attention, wanting to joke around with him. They didn't want to hear about a trip. They were too young to appreciate it. So we did whatever the kids wanted. I figured I had plenty of time to hear about his trip.

Mike wanted to know about our two weeks, about what we had done while he was gone. Well, I had been busy working and bringing Kyle to kung fu class and the girls to dance class. I was also doing my Avon fundraiser for Trinity Catholic Academy, the girls' school. The fundraiser took a lot of my time because I had to write up and submit all the orders. On Saturday night, my sister Linda had come over and asked the girls if they wanted to sleep over at her house. The girls were all excited and said yes. I was shocked, because they had never slept anywhere but home before. Mike was in shock when I told him. He asked if they had made it through the night, and I said yes. The girls had packed their clothes and taken their favorite stuffed animal, Barney, with them.

I'd said to Linda, "This will be nice. I will have some time alone with Kyle. I'm going to take him out to eat." I had let Kyle pick anywhere he wanted to go, and he picked Piccadilly Pub. We were seated in a corner table near a window and had a really nice time talking about him and his sports. Kyle did every sport he could possibly do each season, which kept us very busy. Mike thought it was great that Kyle and I had spent some time together. Since the girls were only three and five years old, I didn't get much special time alone with my son.

The kids were done eating and wanted to go home. We didn't get to do much shopping, but that was okay. We had a good time just being together. About 6:15 p.m., we went outside in the rain and climbed into our blue Dodge Caravan. The girls hopped into the back seat, Katie in the middle and Kimberly on the right side of her. Kyle chose to sit in the middle seat behind his father. Mike was driving, and I was the passenger. Kyle was still thrilled about his autographs and Rollerblades. He put them on the floor next to him, thanking his father for taking him to the mall.

As we started to exit the mall parking lot, I put on the CD that Mike had made me for my birthday. I said, "I played this so much during the two weeks while you were gone. I just love it. It made the time being away from you easier, hearing your voice." He just smiled and said he had missed me and was so happy to be home.

The rain kept coming down hard, and then it would stop and sprinkle. We had planned to stop at my parent's house but decided to go straight home because of the weather. Besides, the kids were tired. We were halfway down Route 20, almost at the Oxford line, and Mike was talking about his trip. As we were going around a corner in the slow lane, we both noticed a truck coming up Route 20 on the opposite side. The truck was crossing into our lane! It happened so fast. The truck came right at us. I heard Mike yell, "Oh my God!" Then I saw his hands go up from the steering wheel.

I woke up, and the dashboard was on my left arm. All I could see was steam. I was in shock, yelling to Mike and the kids, but there was no answer. I kept yelling, and finally Kimberly answered and started to cry. I told her it was okay and asked how Katie was. She said okay, and finally Katie cried out. I told them to sit still, that I was going to try to get to them. But I couldn't move I was trapped. I yelled for Kyle but got no answer. I couldn't even see him. I kept saying, "Mike, answer me. Are you okay?" He didn't answer, and I couldn't see him either. I had a terrible feeling.

Someone was at my door. It was Mike's cousin Cliff and a man I didn't know named Steve. Cliff and Steve tried to get me out, but they couldn't get the door open. Cliff was in shock when he realized who I was and that the driver was his cousin Michael. He went over to Mike to see if he could help him but realized that Mike was already gone. He had passed away!

I was screaming, wanting to know if Mike and Kyle were okay. Someone told me that Kyle and the girls were going to the hospital that Kyle was going into surgery. All I knew was that they were alive, but I still had no word on Mike. I kept yelling to the paramedics to check on Mike, and I was told that he was trapped in the van and no one knew anything.

I remember feeling the rain. My left arm felt like a balloon. I was so scared. All I could hear were sirens and ambulances, and I saw lights flashing. A woman came to me and said, "You need to call your family." I said I would call my parents, but then my mind went blank, and I couldn't remember their phone number. Then I said to call my sister Laurie, and the woman dialed the number. Laurie picked up, and I told her we had been in an accident and were going to the hospital. After that, the women spoke to Laurie and told her where they were taking us. They put me in an ambulance with another women who had hit our car afterward. I hadn't realized that another car was involved. I felt bad that she had run into us, and I apologized to her, hoping that she wasn't hurt. She told me she was okay. They took me to Saint Vincent's in Worcester and my three children to U-Mass in Worcester.

Unbelievably, we had family at the scene of the accident. Clifford and Russell were Mike's cousins, who had been on their way to a state police-boxing tournament to watch a friend compete with thirteen other people. They had been driving in three separate vehicles. While driving up Route 20, they had seen a pickup truck drive past them at seventy to seventy-five miles per hour, so fast that it had startled the guys. They had all been talking about how crazy it was to be driving so fast on Route 20, especially in the rain. When they crossed the town line from Charlton to Oxford and went around a corner, they noticed that the speeding truck had been in an accident.

They had decided to stop and help. Steve and Cliff had gone to the driver's side and realized that Mike couldn't be helped, as the airbag/ steering wheel/dashboard had all compressed against him. Cliff went to Kyle, took him out of the car, and laid him on the ground. It was very dark, with no streetlights, and the little light they had was a flashlight and a light from the van. Once the light was on Kyle, Cliff recognized him as his cousin Mike's son.

Cliff and Steve noticed that Kyle had black mucus coming out of his mouth and ear. Steve knew it wasn't blood, and Kyle was making gurgling sounds like he was choking, so Steve stuck his fingers in Kyle's mouth to try to clear a way for him to breath. Kyle's teeth were clenched tight. An ambulance came and rushed Kyle to U-Mass Hospital. He was only breathing three breaths a minute.

The girls were trapped in the back of the van. Cliff and Steve took the girls out through the broken window, and a woman stopped and put both of the girls in her car, out of the rain. The girls were in shock, and when the paramedics arrived for the girls, they noticed that Katie had a leg problem. Her leg was out of its socket, and she was screaming in pain. The paramedic popped it back into place, and Katie stopped crying and said thank you. Kimberly was in shock, very nervous, and could hardly speak. She hadn't broken any bones, but she had been traumatized.

Mike's brother Norman, a police officer at the time, got a call to go to the scene. He had no idea his brother had just been in a fatal accident with his family. Norman got out of his cruiser, and his cousin Russell stopped him from going to the vehicle. Norman asked, "How bad is it?" Russell said, "Your brother didn't make it." Norman was in shock. He had been to many accidents and had seen so much, but this time it was different. It was his family. Norman asked about the kids and myself. Russell told him that Mike's kids were alive and were all going to U-Mass but that Kyle was in tough shape.

Norman had to get himself together and figure out how he was going to tell his seventy-eight-year-old mother that a drunk driver had just killed her youngest son and that her three grandchildren were badly hurt. Mike's mom, Rita, had already buried two husbands and lost two other sons. She had been through so much in her life already; that Norman knew this was going to destroy her. Norman got into his cruiser, unable to believe that he had lost his baby brother and best friend. Mike and Norman had been together every day. They had been so close and had shared so much.

Norman went to Uncle Ronald and Aunt Gloria's house first. Ronald knew something bad had happened; he could tell by Norman's face. Norman told him that Mike had been killed in a car accident. Ronald was so upset that he threw his cup across the room, tearful and shocked. Norman asked them to come with him to tell his mom, Gloria's sister, who lived right across the street from them.

When they arrived at Rita's house, Norman said, "Mom, sit down. I have to tell you something." She said, "Tell me what's wrong!" and started to cry. Norman told her that Mike had been killed in a car accident and that the kids and myself had been rushed to Worcester. Rita was devastated, in shock, wondering how this could happen. How could she have lost another son? A mom wasn't supposed to bury her children, especially her baby boy.

Ronald and Gloria started to make phone calls to tell Mike's brother and sisters that they had lost their brother. They all started to come down to their mother's house. Everyone was in shock, trying to figure out what had happened and the condition of myself and the children. Rumors were spreading around town fast, and people were saying that

Kyle had passed away also. Mike's family was all together, trying to comfort each other and make sense of it all.

I was brought to a different hospital from my children. I was taken to Saint Vincent's, and the kids were taken to U-Mass. My sister Laurie had called my parents and told them that we had been in an accident and to go to U-Mass. They went immediately, shocked and devastated, not knowing the condition of the kids or myself, but knowing that Mike had been killed. They arrived at the hospital and were told that I had been taken to Saint Vincent's, so my father went to be with me, and my mother stayed at U-Mass to help make decisions for the kids.

The doctor approached my mother and said that Kyle was in very bad condition and that they didn't think he would make it. He had a severe brain injury with five cranial bleeds. They wanted to know if she would give permission to do surgery. They emphasized to her that he might not survive the surgery, but it was their only hope. They said Dr. McGillicuddy would be the surgeon and Kyle was in the best of hands. She told them to do whatever they needed to do, crying hysterically. She loved Kyle and didn't want to lose her grandson.

At first my girls were put on beds in the hallway, with Katie screaming in pain. They had to settle her down and get X-rays of her leg. Mike's cousin Michelle came with her husband Dom to the emergency room, and they were trying to comfort the girls. Dom was hugging Kimberly, and she was so traumatized that she vomited all over Dom. They felt helpless in trying to comfort the girls.

My dad came to me at Saint Vincent's. I was in and out of it. Tears came down his cheeks as he told me how much he loved me and that everything would be okay. The nurses cut off my clothes and checked me for injuries. I kept asking them about my husband and the kids, but they all said they didn't know anything. They wanted me to stay calm. They took me into a room to sew my thumb back on. I was so traumatized, I had no idea what Dr. Morgan was doing to my thumb. I remember looking at the door, and Uncle Ronald, Aunt Gloria, and Aunt Lorraine were there, telling me they loved me and that they were there for me. I could tell that they were all crying.

In my mind, I knew Mike had died. I felt it. I felt so empty. I just needed someone to confirm it to me. Finally the doctor told my dad that he could tell me.

My dad was crying. He loved Mike so much, and they had just gotten back from a trip to England the day before. My dad cried as he said, "Mike passed away." I had known it in my heart, but now it was real. My worst fear had come true. My loving husband, my best friend, was gone. I was given medication for pain and to keep me calm. I couldn't stay awake.

Later on, my sister Laurie and my brother-in-law John came to see me. I was sitting up, crying as I told them that Mike was gone. I had lost my husband. What was I going to do without my husband? Laurie said, "I know. You have us, and we all love you." But I kept saying, "It's not the same. I want my husband. I need him! My brother-in-law hugged me and told me he would always be there for the kids and me.

I had shattered the humerus bone of my left arm. The doctors thought my arm would have to be amputated and said I needed to go into surgery, but my dad asked if I could go to U-Mass to be with my kids. He explained to them that my son was in surgery and that the doctors didn't think he would make it and that my little girls were only three and five and needed me. The doctors at Saint Vincent's agreed that I should go to U-Mass, and I would have the surgery in the morning.

Mike had been trapped in the van. The dashboard and steering wheel had crushed him, and his seat had fallen through the floor. The Jaws of Life was used to take the roof off the van to get him out. Norman called Sansoucy Funeral home, and they picked Mike up and brought him to Boston. When a person gets into an accident like this, the authorities have to do an autopsy to see how the person died and to check for alcohol and drugs.

Chapter 5

In the middle of the night, not really knowing what was happening, I was told that I was being transferred to U-Mass. My parents met with Dr. Yvonne Shelton, and the doctor said they might have to amputate my arm, but my father begged the doctor to try to save it. My father just couldn't accept that, telling the doctor how hard it would be for me with my kids being so young and my son being so injured. The doctors said they would do their best, but the bone had been shattered, and they weren't sure if it could be saved.

I remember going into surgery, in and out of consciousness, with the mask over my face, not knowing what was happening to me. I only knew that I was in a hospital and was having surgery. I remember that during the surgery they woke me up and asked me if I could move my fingers. I did, very little, and I'll never forget the laughter and clapping in the operating room. I still had no idea what was happening.

When I woke up, they explained what happened to my arm. They told me that I had shattered my humerus bone and that it was a miracle that they had saved my arm. They'd had to use two plates and fifteen-plus screws to hold my humerus bone together. The doctor said it would take a full year to recover, with a lot of physical and occupational therapy, and the nerve had to regrow from my shoulder to my fingers. I was so thankful that I had my arm, but there was so much happening with Kyle that I wanted to know about him and the girls.

My whole family was at the hospital. Everyone was trying to help with the girls and comfort me. It was overwhelming, but I was so thankful that they were there for me. I was told that my sister Diane was flying home from Washington State. I was happy, as I loved all my sisters so much, and I knew that I needed them more than ever. I knew they would do anything for me, as we were all very close.

Dr. Jonathan Wood came to talk to me about Kyle's injuries. He told me that Kyle was a lucky boy to make it through the surgery but that he was in very tough shape. The doctor explained that he'd had a very bad head injury with five cranial bleeds, left subdural hematoma and a small bowel resection from the seatbelt. He'd also had two strokes and was in a coma. He told me that Kyle couldn't breathe on his own, and Dr. Wood wasn't sure if he ever would. Kyle was in critical condition, and the next twenty-four hours were very important. There would be lots of medical decisions ahead of us. They were keeping a very close watch on him, taking MRIs and CAT scans often.

I couldn't believe what I was hearing about my ten-year-old boy, a happy little guy with so much energy, a boy so active in sports and so loving. How could this be happening? No one could ask for a better son. I thought, *this has to be a bad dream. I can't lose my son. I just lost my husband!* I had to get myself together and be strong. Kyle and the girls needed me more than ever. I couldn't focus on losing Mike. I had to put that aside and focus on the kids.

I asked to see Kyle, and they said yes, preparing me before I went in. The nurse told me they'd had to shave Kyle's head and put a breathing tube in his mouth and a feeding tube in his nose. He had an IV, oxygen, and a heart monitor. I just listened and was overwhelmed. The nurse brought me to him in a wheelchair, as I could barely walk. I had hematomas all over my legs, my back was injured, and my arm was in a cast. But I just wanted to see my son.

I arrived at Kyle's room, scared to go in, but I needed to see my baby boy. The nurse wheeled me to Kyle's side. I got to hold his hand and to tell him how much I loved him and that he needed to fight and stay strong. He looked so different with no hair, with tape all over his face to hold the tubes. Kyle's nurse Martha Wilkins explained to me what were happening and what all the machines were? She was very pleasant and very nurturing. Martha said she would be in here keeping a close eye on Kyle. I just couldn't believe that this was happening. The nurse wouldn't let me stay too long because I was so drugged up. They needed me to get stronger. The nurse told me they had a room down the hall for my girls and me, so we could all be together. She said I could visit Kyle later on, but now she would take me to see my girls. I was so happy to be able to go see them. I needed to see for myself that they were alive and okay.

The nurse wheeled me down the hall to my huge room. The room was packed with family, and I was so happy they were taking care of my girls. My girls started to cry when they saw me. Kim was able to sit in bed with me, but Katie was in so much pain that she was in a crib and couldn't be taken out. I tried to stand by the crib, but I didn't last long. I was too weak. Her crib stood right next to my bed, and we put the bed and crib close together so we could hold hands. Katie seemed to be happy with that. Kim's bed was across the room, but she could come to lie down with me, which was so nice.

I could tell that Kim was very traumatized, not knowing what had happened to her father and brother. She never asked about it, either. When she tried to speak, she couldn't get the sounds out, and this made her even more frustrated. Katie was in so much pain with her injured femur that she cried a lot. Her leg was in a sling as she lay flat on her back. It was really tough. My sisters and Mike's family would read to the kids, comforting them in any way they could. They also spent time with Kyle, so he wasn't alone either. Everyone worked together and helped out as much as they could.

From my bed, I told my sister Patty to call Kyle Sr., Kyle's biological father. I said that he must have heard about the accident, and I asked Patty to tell him that he could come to see Kyle but that he wasn't allowed to go into his room. Kyle hadn't seen him in over a year, and I didn't know if he could hear anything. Kyle was so fragile that I was afraid he might go into cardiac arrest if he heard his biological father's voice. I couldn't risk upsetting Kyle in any way, as his body needed to heal.

I also told Patty that I didn't want to see Kyle Sr. myself. I had no reason to ever talk or see him again. Please explain to him it's only to see little Kyle.

My sister called Kyle Sr. and told him about little Kyle and the accident he'd been in. He came to the hospital, looked through the window, and talked to the doctors and my family. I felt good, knowing that he came. If something happened to little Kyle, at least he would've gotten to look at him one last time. I knew he loved him in his own way, but just couldn't figure it all out.

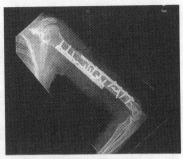

*Our mini van after the
car accident, 1997.*

*Lisa's left arm after her
humorous was shattered.*

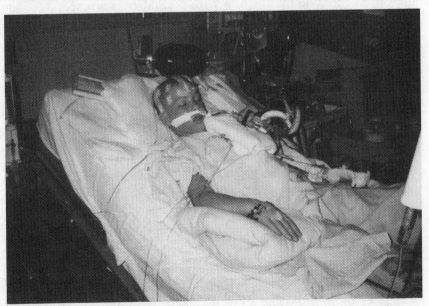

Kyle, 10 years old, in a coma and on a ventilator for 7 weeks.

Chapter 6

As I lay in bed with everyone else sleeping, much was going through my mind. Turning my head, I looked at Katie's and Kimberly's innocent faces and felt so bad for all the pain they were in, knowing there wasn't anything I could do for any of my three children. I was afraid for the girls to wake up, realizing that I had to tell them the truth about their daddy and brother. Their little hearts would be shattered even more than they were already.

The girls were wondering about their daddy and brother, and I just couldn't believe that I had to tell them they would never see their daddy again. They were too young for this. How were they going to grow up without a daddy? Mike had been so close to his kids. Every night, he gave the girls their bath and then played on the floor with all three of the children. He tucked them in and told them bedtime stories or practiced the numbers on the clock. He had so loved the kids. I could only hope to carry on that love during the years ahead of them, always reminding them that their daddy was watching over all of us, that he was still with us, only in a different way.

I rang for the nurse and asked if I could go to see Kyle. She brought me a wheelchair and rolled me down the hall to see him. After I held Kyle's warm hand for a bit, his doctor came in and said he would like to have a meeting with my family and me to discuss Kyle's injuries. We set a time for later that day. I sat there with Kyle, just looking at his handsome face, unable to understand how we had all been so happy only two days ago. How could this be my little ten-year-old? From what the doctor's were saying, I knew the prognosis wasn't good, but I felt in my heart that I wasn't going to lose him. I *couldn't* lose him!

My brother David asked Father DiOrio to visit Kyle and me. I knew of Father DiOrio, as my parents often went to his masses, but I'd never met him before. I'll never forget the first time this priest entered Kyle's room. He came over to me, put his healing hands over me, and prayed for me to be healed and to believe in God to give me the strength I needed. I remember shaking so much, but I was also relieved that he was there. I knew he was a good man and that the good Lord worked miracles through him. It gave me so much hope.

As Kyle lay there, it was so quiet that we could hear the machines running. Father DiOrio put his healing hands on Kyle's head and started to pray. He took out his blessed oil and put it all over Kyle's body. Then he gave Kyle a cross, which we kept taped to his hand at all times.

I can't even describe the peace I felt, knowing that someone so close to our Jesus was with Kyle and me. I felt positive that no matter what happened, it would be okay, because I knew Kyle was a little angel. If God wanted him, I knew Kyle would be in a better place, and I knew he would be with his daddy. However, even though I knew that, I still couldn't believe I would lose Kyle. I had so much hope. I prayed and prayed. Father DiOrio tapped me on the shoulder, said he would be back tomorrow, and left.

I went back to my room. I knew the girls would be waking up, and I wanted to be there for them. The nurse helped me back into bed, and I asked her for some pain medicine, as my arm was hurting badly. I didn't want to take anything too strong, because I needed to be alert to talk to my girls and make decisions for Kyle.

Kimberly woke up and said, "Hi, Mommy." I said, "Can you come lie with me in my bed?" She jumped out of bed and came over and gave me the biggest hug! I told her everything would be okay and that I loved her very much. She was trying to talk, but she had a lot of trouble because her anxiety was really bad. She was trying to ask me when she could see Daddy and Kyle. I said, "When Katie wakes up, after breakfast, we will talk about that."

She just nodded and stayed close to me and asked what had happened to my arm. I explained that my arm was broken but would be okay and that I wasn't in much pain. "Don't worry about Mommy," I told her. "I will be fine."

"Why can't you walk?" she asked.

I said, "When we were in the car accident, I got all bruised up, and my legs hurt. But each day it will get better, and I will walk." I wanted to change the subject, so I said, "What are we going to have for breakfast?" She started to think about it, and then Katie started to wake up.

Katie looked at me with her gorgeous blue eyes and tangled blonde hair and said, "I want you to hold me. I need you, Mommy!" It was so sad. She was in a crib with her leg up in a harness, so I couldn't hold her. I leaned over her crib as much as I could, but with my arm broken, it was difficult. She said, "It's okay, Mommy. I know you can't. Just hold my hand." We ordered breakfast, and then company started to come.

My brother-in-law Norman came to see me. He looked tired and drained, mourning the loss of his brother as he realized that this nightmare was reality. He had lost his baby brother, his best friend, but he was helping his mother and siblings and was trying to make decisions about Mike's funeral.

Norman handed me a CD. It was the CD of Mike singing, the CD that had been playing in the van the night of the accident; the one Mike had made me for my thirtieth birthday party. Norman said, "They saved it." I was so thankful, because that CD was so special to me—now more than ever.

Norman told me that Mike had to have an autopsy in Boston, and he'd had Sansoucy Funeral Home pick him up. We talked about Mike's funeral. Norman said that if Mike were going to be shown, they would have to do the funeral without me. I was going to be in the hospital for ten days, and we were already on the third day. If they waited for me to be released from the hospital, they probably couldn't show him. I said I didn't care. I wasn't missing my husband's funeral, and they were going to have to wait for me. Norman was fine with that and told me not to worry about anything. He said he would do everything that needed to be done.

Norman asked me where I wanted Mike to be buried. I said I wanted him to be where his family was. Norman said he would check it out and see if there was anything close by. I told him to pick out the best casket, and I told him which suit to put his brother in. I was so thankful that he was handling this for me, because I knew how much he loved his brother and would do only the best for him.

It was time for the meeting about Kyle, and my parents, Uncle Ronald, Aunt Gloria, and a few of my sisters were there. Dr. Wood took out MRI images and explained Kyle's brain injury. The frontal lobe and cerebellum were severely damaged. There was a lot of gray color in the film; it was overwhelming. The doctor said that if Kyle lived, he would be in a vegetative state, that he most likely wouldn't know any of us. He explained that there was a fluid buildup on Kyle's brain and that they needed to operate and put in a shunt.

I remember asking what a shunt would do. Dr. Wood explained, "Fluid is building up and has no place to go, so it's putting pressure on the brain, which will deflate the brain. A shunt, which is like a straw, will create a passage where the fluid can drain and then the pressure wouldn't be on his brain. This will help Kyle to recover and to be more alert. The drainage will go into his heart. Normally it would be attached to his stomach, but we can't do that at this time. The left side of his stomach was damaged from the seat belt. Dr. Thomas Cohen performed a small bowel resection, surgery, Kyle's intestines has to heal from the inside out. He can't have any type of food or fluid in his stomach. When we give Kyle nutrition through his nose, it flows to a point below the stomach." I asked Dr. Wood when they would be putting in the shunt, and the doctor replied, "Later this afternoon Dr. Robin Davidson will be doing the surgery."

I was terrified, but I knew I had to stay focused, and I was thankful that there was a surgery that could help him. The doctors said that Kyle would be like a vegetable. I had heard the term before, but I couldn't believe it. Putting that thought aside, I focused on getting through Kyle's surgery and telling my girls about Kyle and their daddy.

I went to see Kyle, staying with him for a while until he was taken to surgery. I gave him a kiss and told him that his daddy and I loved him very much. I told him that his sisters were waiting for him to get better. No one is really sure if a person in a coma can hear or understand, but I had to tell Kyle, just in case. I felt that he could hear me. They took Kyle off to surgery, and I went back in my wheelchair to see my girls.

When I entered my room, I saw lots of family and friends there. The girls were good, there was no screaming, and Katie had pain meds. I decided it was a good time to talk to my girls. I didn't want them to hear about their dad from anyone else. I needed to tell them myself. I asked the nurse if there was any way Katie could be closer to me. We put the beds as close together as we could and rose up my hospital bed as far as it would go. Kimberly sat in my bed with me.

I asked if everyone could leave the room so I could talk to my girls alone. Everyone left quietly, because they knew what I was going to tell the girls. I tried to be calm and strong. Holding Kimberly as much as I could and gripping Katie's hand, I told my girls I had something very important to talk to them about. Their big, blue eyes got bigger as they both looked at me. I said, "Do you remember the car accident?" They both said yes. Katie said, "That's why I'm in so much pain. I hurt my leg." I said, "Yes, and in time, that will get better, just like my arm will."

I told the girls that Kyle had hurt his head very badly and that he was sleeping in a room down the hall. They wanted to know if they could see him. I said, "I will take you to see him, but we can only look through the window. Kyle needs to rest and heal." I tried to explain that there were a lot of machines around him and that they'd had to shave Kyle's head. The girls took that pretty well. They just wanted to see him. Since Kyle was in surgery, I told them that I would take them to see Kyle tomorrow, and they were happy.

"Daddy was injured very badly too," I said. Kim said anxiously, "Yeah, Daddy had a red hat on. I could see his head." I knew that Mike hadn't been wearing a red hat, so I figured he must have cut his head, and the blood must have been so bad that Kim had thought it was a hat. I said, "Daddy had some big boo-boos that couldn't be healed. Daddy died, and now he is an angel with God." Being only three and five years old, the girls were confused and asked, "Can we see Daddy?" I said, "No, we will never see him again. Your daddy loves us, but he will be with us in a different way."

The girls started screaming. "No! I want my daddy! I want my daddy!" We were all crying. It was just awful. With the girls being so little, all I could do was comfort them as much as I could. I couldn't even hold them properly. I could only hold Katie's little hand as Kim hugged my neck tight. After we all calmed down, family members came back in and tried to distract the girls, playing games with Kim and reading a story to Katie.

It was a tough and draining day, but much was accomplished. Kyle made it through surgery, and I got to visit him later that night. While I was there, he had a seizure. His body starting shaking badly, and I yelled for Martha the nurse. Kyle was given medication to keep any seizures under control. He ended up having two episodes, but after that night, we never saw any more seizures.

Once Kyle was settled, I went back to my hospital room to see my girls. It had been a hard day for all of us, and I thought about what had taken place that day. I'd had a wonderful visit with Father DiOrio; I had made plans for Mike's funeral; I'd had a meeting with the doctors; Kyle had survived major surgery; and I'd told my girls about their daddy dying and about Kyle's condition. And the night had ended with Kyle having two major seizures.

I was so overwhelmed, I remember talking to Mike, saying "How am I going to do this without you? I need you so much right now. I need you to help me make decisions for Kyle." I prayed that my little boy would not be taken from me. More than anything, I needed him to survive. I couldn't lose both of them. Then I cried myself to sleep.

Chapter 7

When my eyes opened and I realized it was morning, I was afraid of what the day was going to bring. It didn't take long before the doctor came into my room to talk about Katie's leg. He had decided that they needed to put Katie in a body cast. A body cast? I asked what that was. He explained that it was a cast that would go from her chest down to her feet. It would be very uncomfortable for her and would possibly get itchy, but it was the only way to heal her femur. She needed to stay still and not move for two months. I said that two months was a long time for a three-year-old.

The doctor said that Katie would pretty much have to be in a lying-down position. I asked how she would go to the bathroom. He said that the clinician would leave an opening in the cast for her, and someone would have to lift her to put her on the potty. We would need a commode for our home. I couldn't help but think how hard it would be to lift Katie, especially with the weight of a full cast. However, with help from both sides of the family, I knew we would somehow make it work.

A nurse brought in a doll with a body cast on to show Katie what she was going to look like. Katie was okay with it when the nurse told her it wouldn't hurt to put the cast on. The doctor told Katie she could pick out any color she wanted for her cast, and she loved that. Later that day, she got her cast on, and she picked the color purple. Kimberly was the first person to sign her cast. Katie was such a big girl and handled it well. Katie's pain was more controlled now, so she wasn't screaming as much. This was a blessing for me, as I felt helpless about her pain. It also helped Kimberly to see that her sister was getting better.

Kyle was still in critical condition, in a coma, not responding. He had a fever, and a test showed that he had a staph infection. That meant that he had to have surgery to remove the shunt and put in another kind. I just couldn't believe that my poor child was going to have his fourth surgery in just four days. His body was fighting an infection—on top of his brain hemorrhages and a bowel resection that was trying to heal. How much more could his little body take? Would he make it through this? I prayed, hoping that he could survive this nightmare that we were in. I kissed my helpless son good-bye again before he left for surgery. The situation was killing me. I cried and cried.

My sister Diane arrived from Washington State. It was nice to have her home, and I was thankful that she kept Kyle company day and night. She read and prayed to God for healing to overcome Kyle's injuries and for the strength he needed to survive. Both sides of my family and many friends were with us. My children and I were so blessed to have so many people around us. It helped so much to be able to talk and to share my feelings.

Katie was doing well in her body cast. It was a little itchy, but she was handling it. Kimberly still had trouble speaking, and the doctor said it could linger on for a long while. We needed to have patience with her and give her the time she needed to speak.

Kyle returned from surgery after doing well again. He was back in his room in the intensive care unit. Later that night, I decided to take the girls to visit Kyle, but only to look through the window. The girls needed to see that Kyle was alive. We put Katie in a wheelchair that reclined, because she could not sit up. Kimberly sat with me in my wheelchair. We were wheeled down to Kyle's room, where we looked through a big window at their brother. I explained that he was sleeping and that the machines were helping him to breathe. They yelled to Kyle that they loved him and said they were going to color him a picture. They were so sweet and acted so mature for their ages. I was so proud of them for the way they handled the situation. We went back to our room, and they colored pictures for Kyle.

We were all exhausted from another day of hell and decisions. My pain was getting worse, especially in my back, and the bruises on my legs were now big and black. My sister Linda would rub my back for me whenever she was around, which helped with the pain. Father DiOrio called and said he was sorry he couldn't visit that day, but he would come tomorrow. He asked me if there was anything I needed. I said, "I need strength. Please pray for strength—and for Kyle. He wasn't good, and the doctors still aren't sure if he'll make it." He told me good night and said he would see me in the morning.

I fell asleep around 11:00 or so that night. When I felt someone touch my forehead, I immediately woke up and saw Father DiOrio at my bedside. For a second, I thought I had passed away, but he immediately said, "It's okay, Lisa. It's Father DiOrio. Jesus told me I should come down now. You needed me, so I am here. Rest. I am going to pray for strength and a healing from our Jesus." While he was saying a prayer for me, a doctor came in and said, "Kyle isn't doing well. His body is shutting down. You need to call your family and come to Kyle's room." Father DiOrio went immediately to Kyle's room, and the nurse got me up. I was numb with shock. Had they just told me that Kyle was dying? That couldn't be true. I couldn't lose him!

The nurse called my family, and they started to arrive. Everyone was hugging each other and crying. When I arrived at Kyle's room, Father DiOrio was praying over him. I was in awe. He prayed over Kyle for a while and then stepped into the hallway. I was talking to Kyle's doctor when Father DiOrio came to me and said, "What do you want from Kyle?" I thought, *what does he mean?* Father DiOrio said, "How do you want your son to be?"

Dr. Wood said, "He is going to die. He will not make it through the night." Father said that Kyle would live, and then he asked me again what I would like. I was so confused! I thought, *the doctor says that Kyle is dying, and if he lives, he will be a vegetable. Father says that Kyle won't die, and he's asking what I want.* I said, "I want my son to know me. I want to make him happy. I want to know his wants and needs." Father DiOrio looked right at me and said, "You will have that."

I went to Kyle's bedside and held his hand. Dr. Wood again explained to me that Kyle's body was shutting down, that he wouldn't make it through the night. I held Kyle's hand and kissed him. I stopped crying and said to Kyle firmly, "We need to make a decision. If you decide to go with Daddy, it's okay. Daddy will take care of you. But I want you to know that if you decide to stay here with your mom and your sisters, we will be with you every step of the way. I promise you that I will never leave you, and we will make it!" Then I told Kyle how much I loved him.

After a few minutes, the machines started registering activity. Kyle's body was coming back! The doctors and nurses couldn't believe what was happening. Jesus had given me a miracle! Kyle had decided he wanted to stay. I truly believe in my heart that Kyle had gone to his daddy and that his daddy wanted him to come back to his sisters and me because he knew I couldn't bear to lose Kyle. How could I have functioned after losing both of them?

That night I fervently thanked Jesus and Mike for letting me keep my son!

Chapter 8

Walking through the halls in the Pedi ICU unit, I saw so many rooms filled with sick or injured kids. As I walked by, I noticed parents crying and families holding each other. It's a sad environment. I wouldn't wish this on any parent. One thing we all had in common was we wanted our loved ones to get better. The staff at U-Mass Hospital was great; everyone was so nice and friendly. My family and I were treated with respect, and they took the time to listen to our concerns and answer all of our questions. This helped me learn to trust them—especially Kyle's nurse Martha. I knew Kyle was in great hands under Martha's care. She was always so sweet, and took the time to explain everything to me, and believe me I was full of questions. She was my angel.

I arrived at Kyle's room, and Martha was by his bedside. He was breathing very hard, his chest rising very high and fast. Martha said she had just paged the doctor. I had no idea what was happening to him or why his breathing was so loud. Dr. Wood came and examined Kyle and took some tests. He said that we would have a meeting when the test results came back.

I knew it was serious, so I called my parents and some of my sisters, who were already at the hospital. What could this be? So much was going through my mind. Was I going to lose Kyle now? I started shaking uncontrollably. I held Kyle's hand, and tried to calm him, but nothing worked.

The doctor received the test results, and we went into a huge room with a big table and chairs. We all sat down, and Dr. Wood explained to us that Kyle's brain stem had shifted, and his brain was telling him to breathe like this. He said the only way to fix his breathing was to do a tracheostomy. He also suggested that we put in a feeding tube. Being fed through the nose (Nasogastric tube) long-term wasn't good. It could cause an infection.

I couldn't believe what I was hearing: a feeding tube and tracheotomy? I came right out and said, "I don't think he needs a tracheotomy, and I will not do a feeding tube. It's way too soon. I want to give him more time to wake up and get stronger. The doctor said, "Think about it. The tracheotomy is the only way to stop this. He could breathe like this for the rest of his life—or until the brain stem moves again."

I went back into Kyle's room. His breathing was so loud. How much more could he take? And what about his heart? Father DiOrio was called in. He went over to Kyle, put his hands on Kyle's neck, and tilted his head backward a little—and the loud breathing stopped! What had just happened? Dr. Wood was there, and he checked Kyle and said, "Well, I guess he will have to stay with his neck back, then. Otherwise, if we move his head forward, the heavy breathing will start again." We left Kyle's head tilted back for a while. I never thought the noise of the machines alone would sound so good.

As Father DiOrio left, I thanked him so much for coming. He told me that Kyle would be okay, and I believed him. It was a miracle! My sister Patty and I talked about the feeding tube. Her daughter had one, and she said, "Lisa, follow your gut. I think it's too early also. Give it time." If Kyle was going to live, I wanted him to be able to breathe and eat on his own. He hadn't been born like this, and I didn't want machines and formula keeping him alive. I wanted to give Kyle more time to wake from his coma before I decided on a tracheotomy and feeding tube. Since he didn't have any infection from the feeding tube in his nose, I felt like I had time. Why rush into it?

I told Dr. Wood of my decision not to do either surgery. He said that was okay, but he advised me to go and get guardianship of my children, just in case. If I had been at a Catholic hospital, I probably wouldn't have been able to refuse the surgery. I said, "Guardianship? He's my child!" The doctor insisted that I needed to do this, so I contacted a lawyer to get one for all three of my children. I was shocked that I even had to do such a thing.

I went back to see Kyle. Dr. Wood had shifted Kyle's head position back to normal, and there was no heavy breathing. I felt so relieved, and the doctor was surprised. Kyle was always full of surprises. It was a miracle that he was still with us. I kissed my son and went back to my own hospital room. I was exhausted, and I took some pain meds. I needed a break.

Chapter 9

The girls' doctor came in the next day and said that Kimberly could go home. I wasn't happy about that, because Katie and I weren't able to go home yet. I didn't want Kim to be without her sister. I had no choice but to send her home, as insurance wouldn't allow her to stay any longer. I had to explain to her that she got to go home and be with Meme (Mike's mom) and Aunt Jean. Kim handled it very well, because she loved her Meme and Aunt Jean. They lived next to us, so we saw them every day. I knew they would take good care of her.

Katie was having a lot of spasms. Sometimes they would get so bad that she would cry a lot. One time when she was crying, she suddenly started laughing. Aunt Lorraine asked her, "Why are you laughing?" Katie said, "My daddy just came and told me a joke, and he kissed me on the cheek!" Aunt Lorraine and Aunt Gloria were in shock, but Katie was happy, and that was all that mattered.

Kyle was still in a lot of danger. The doctors realized that he had formed a blood clot in his leg. Kyle couldn't have a blood transfusion, because he'd had brain surgery. This meant that he needed surgery again to put in a "greenfield filter screen." My little boy just couldn't get a break. It was one thing after another. He was still in a deep coma. They planned on doing the surgery soon. The shunt was working, the swelling of the brain was going down, and his stomach was healing, but he still had weeks to go. At least he wasn't having any more seizures.

I decided to play Mike's CD for Kyle, knowing how much Kyle loved it. It was my first time hearing Mike's voice since the accident. It instantly brought me to tears, even though it was hard I found it soothing and I hoped Kyle would also.

I had some visitors from United Lens Company: Al, Jim, and Denise. I was so happy to see them. They told me how sorry they were and that they would do anything they could for my family. Al told me he was giving all the employees of United Lens the day off to attend Mike's funeral. I was shocked, because they never shut the company down. They had done so only one other time in the company's history—when Al's father had died. Al respected Mike very much, as Mike had been with UL for twenty-one years and had never once called in sick. Everyone there had loved Mike.

Al also told me that before Mike had gone to England he had changed his life insurance with the company. He had wanted to make sure we would be okay if something happened to him. Al said that Mike had had a feeling that something was going to happen to him. Al told me that when I felt better he would help guide me to the correct financial people. He was as caring as a father would have been. I couldn't believe that Mike had never told me about the change in insurance, but I guess he hadn't wanted me to worry.

Al also told me not to worry about the gathering after the funeral. Everyone was going to go to Rom's restaurant, and Al was picking up the tab. I was so surprised and thankful. Al was such a good man and I respected him so much he passed away August 2010, we were very blessed to have him in our lives, and I will never, ever forget him.

Kyle went again into surgery—this time, for the blood clot—and they told me it wouldn't be a long surgery. I kissed him good-bye again, feeling like that was all I ever did. I couldn't believe how much his little body could take. It was only our fifth day, but I could tell that he was losing weight. Dr. Wood said he was very strong, and his heart and organs were in great shape. Luckily, Kyle hadn't broken any bones. It was all head trauma from going back and forth.

All I could do now was pray for Kyle to get through this surgery. I felt so numb and weak. I just wanted to take all this pain away. If only I could go back to the first day of November and stay home that night, I would still have my husband, and my children wouldn't have this nightmare. As a parent, I felt so helpless. There wasn't anything I could do except pray and think positively.

Chapter 10

It was a big day for Katie and me. We finally got to go home after ten days in the hospital. I was happy for Katie, but I knew it was going to be horrible for me. Kyle was still in a coma, fighting for his life. I was so afraid to leave him. I went to see him before we were discharged, and I told him I would be back sometime tomorrow. I knew that returning home was going to be difficult because my husband was no longer there. Kyle was still in critical condition, and I wouldn't be staying right next door to him any longer.

I just did whatever I had to do. Even though my emotions were running high, I had to stay strong for my kids, and that was what I focused on. I knew that if I let myself get all depressed, I wouldn't make it, and my girls would fall apart.

Katie and I went home by ambulance in the early afternoon. Katie was so happy, even in her body cast. She just wanted to be home and to see her Meme and Aunt Jean and show them what had happened to her. When I got out of the ambulance, I was still in a lot of pain, but I tried to stay steady as I walked to the house. Katie was brought inside on a stretcher.

Kimberly came running to me, and Katie was clearly excited to be home. Meme Rita was there, and we cried and hugged each other tight. I told her how sorry I was. Meme is a very tough and strong person, having handled much tragedy in her life, and she had the attitude that we would be okay. We needed to focus on the kids and get through the next couple of days with the funeral and the wake. I respected and admired Meme's strength, and knowing that she was there helped me to stay strong and focused. Together we would get through this nightmare.

My little apartment was very different, as Aunt Jean had moved everything around. My kitchen table had been placed against the wall, and my living room furniture had been taken to the garage. We needed two hospital beds for Katie and me, and Kimberly's bed had been brought down to the living room also. We needed to be together. I cried as reality set in, realizing what had happened to my little family.

Katie's commode was delivered, and we had to figure out who could lift her onto it. We planned a schedule for taking care of the girls. Both sides of the family were wonderful—including friends and people we didn't even know well. Everyone wanted to help out, whether that meant making food or giving rides.

I had to let my family take over and schedule who was doing what. I knew I would be with Kyle every day, and I couldn't take care of my girls because of my injuries. I wanted to go to my bedroom upstairs. I wanted to lie in my bed, hoping I would feel closer to Mike, hoping his scent would be in the bed sheets, but when I got up there, I realized that the bed had been washed and done over. I cried about it, and Aunt Jean came upstairs, feeling very bad. I said, "You didn't know. It's okay." But deep down I was dying. I just missed and wanted Mike so badly. I needed a hug.

Trying to get myself together for Mike's wake that night, much was going through my mind. I was a complete mess. I needed to take a shower, pick out clothes, and gather the strength to get through this tough night ahead. All I knew was that I wanted to see Mike, and I wanted time alone with him.

I went to take a shower and realized that I had to have a bath because of my cast. We wrapped it all up in plastic, and a family member helped me get in and wash my hair. I felt helpless, and now that my family had to wash me, all my pride went out the window. I said to myself that my family didn't mind helping me. They loved me and were trying to help. And I needed the help. I couldn't do it without them. It got easier after a few times, but getting up from the tub was very hard on me. My legs were bruised and aching with pain.

My friend Sharon volunteered to stay with the girls while I went to the wake with my family. I was happy that she offered, because my girls loved her, and I knew they were in good hands with her. My parents came to take me to the funeral home. I told the girls that Mommy was going out for a little bit and would be home that night. Sharon was going to read to them and play games with them. They were fine with that and kissed me good-bye. They were so young, yet so mature for their young ages. Kimberly was just happy to have her little sister back home with her. I am a very lucky mother to be so blessed with my two beautiful daughters.

We left for Sansoucy Funeral Home, and Mike's family was right behind us. The hours at the funeral home were from four to eight p.m. I arrived at three p.m., as I wanted time alone with Mike. I walked into the room where Mike was resting, and I was overwhelmed. So many people were already there, and a line was forming outside. I looked at Norman and said, "I need everyone to leave the room. I want time alone with Mike." Tears started to roll down my face. Norman cleared the room and shut the door behind me.

Finally, I was with the man of my dreams. I went up to the casket, trying to be strong. I put my hand on his head and rubbed his hair. It was so fine and thin. I noticed he had a severe cut on the back of his head. I knew instantly that Kimberly had been right. He had been bleeding badly, which was why she'd said he had a red hat on. I hugged and kissed him. I felt his suit over his stomach area, but all I could feel was tissue. He looked just like Mike, so handsome, dressed in his favorite suit.

Tears came down my cheeks as I told him how much he meant to me; how I would never, ever forget him. I told him he was the best husband I could ever have asked for, that he would always be with me. I thanked him for making the past nine years together so wonderful, and I said that I wouldn't change a thing about it. I thanked him for being such a wonderful father to our children. I promised him I would raise our children to be strong, confident, positive individuals. They would travel and see the world, as he had wanted them to. More importantly, they would know how much he loved them. I would never let them forget their father. Our children would know what a good man and father he had been to them. I asked Mike to guide me, especially with all the decisions ahead concerning Kyle. I needed Mike to be with me and to give me the strength to speak up when needed, to have patience for what was ahead of us.

I heard a knock at the door. Norman came in and said, "Lisa, it's time. We have to start." I had Norman take off Mike's tie. Mike hated neckties. He'd always said that he felt like he was being choked. The family was all lined up to greet family and friends. My father stood by my side, helping me to stand and sit. I was very weak and couldn't stand for long. People came and kept coming. The line seemed never-ending. Everyone gave hugs and offered their sympathy, telling me that Mike would always be with me. So many people cried; there was not a dry eye in the place. I was in tears myself, asking everyone as they passed by to please pray for Kyle. I was told that more than two thousand people came to pay their respects to this wonderful man.

It was early in the morning on the day of the funeral, another hard day. I called the hospital to check on Kyle, and the nurse said that there had been no change. Kyle still had a low-grade fever that he just couldn't break. I told the nurse I was going to try to get there that night after Mike's funeral.

After I hung up the phone, Kimberly came to me and said, "Mommy, look what I found!" It was a tie she had made her daddy for Father's Day that year. It was beautiful. I said, "You know what, Kim? How would you like Daddy to be buried with this tie? She was very excited. I asked her to go find Katie's tie also and something of Kyle's.

When Kimberly came back upstairs, she had Katie's tie and a picture that Kyle had drawn of his famous dog for Daddy. I said, "Perfect." I gave her a big hug and showed Katie. I said, "Daddy will be so happy to have this. It was Daddy's kind of tie." We gathered pictures of us to put with Mike in his casket. The girls were happy that they could give their Daddy something. A therapist who had come to check on the girls had given me a book about death and funerals. The book would help my children to understand where their daddy was resting and what a casket was. I told my girls that tonight I was going to read them a very special book.

When I arrived at the funeral parlor, I placed the ties on Mike and put the pictures and Kyle's drawing with him in his casket. Mike looked like Mike now. Those ties showed who he was—a wonderful father, a true and genuine family man. I still couldn't believe that this was Mike lying there in a casket. This would be the last time I would ever see him again.

We all said our good-byes and went to Notre Dame Church for his mass. My father and I entered through the side door. I was too weak to walk up the stairs and down the long aisle. The church was packed; not a seat could be had, and people were standing along the sides. I had never seen this church so packed. I was overwhelmed by so much love and sadness in one place. So many people had loved Mike. He had been a wonderful man, husband, father, son, brother, uncle, and friend to so many.

I sat in the pew with my parents, and my dad held my hand. I was shaking, staring at Mike's casket, trying to come to a realization that this was for real, that this was happening, that my husband was gone. Looking around, I saw that Mike's family was just as devastated as mine was. I didn't know what to do. I just did what I was supposed to do.

Mike had a beautiful mass, and my sister Gina shared a few words about her brother-in-law, about what a wonderful person he was and how he had loved his family. She said that his children were his life, and he had always been so proud of them, bragging about them often. He had loved his wife, Lisa, and together they had provided a wonderful home for their children. Mike had always been so thoughtful and generous, and all his nieces and nephews were going to miss him. Mike had always made time to play with and listen to each of them. He had always been so wonderful to all five of his sisters-in-law. He had loved them all, and they had given him lots of laughs. His home had been a home to everyone, and many would miss him.

The mass was over. This was it, the last time we would ever be together in this church again. We'd gotten married there and had come to church every week with our kids. Our girls had been baptized there, and Kyle had made his first communion there. So many memories were going through my mind—good ones. But now any future memories with Mike would be no more. How could this be? My father took my arm and said, "We need to go." I got up slowly and walked by Mike's casket, staring at it. I felt like I was going to fall, but my father held me up and walked me slowly down the aisle. There was not a dry eye in the place.

My dad helped me into the funeral procession vehicle, and Aunt Jean sat next to me. We talked about all the people who had come to the funeral, and we agreed that if Mike was looking down on this, he would say, "Unbelievable!" He wouldn't have believed that so many people had come to say good-bye to him.

Then it was time to leave the parking lot at Notre Dame Church. The hearse carrying Mike was in front of my car. We were going to Mike's resting place at the New Notre Dame Cemetery on Woodstock Road. When we arrived at the cemetery, we stayed in the car for a while until everyone else had arrived. The line was endless, and the cemetery was packed solid. Cars had to park along the road, and people had to walk a distance.

I was escorted out of the vehicle and was taken to a chair near Mike's casket. This was really difficult for me. I just couldn't stop crying. I looked up and saw all the sad faces and people feeling so bad, and there was a lot of crying and sniffling. The priest gave the last sermon as I sat there feeling traumatized. One by one, family members placed a rose on Mike's casket before we left. Then it was my turn, and I cried uncontrollably as I placed my red rose on his casket, my father holding me up. I couldn't believe that Mike was gone. How could this be happening?

Jean and I went back into our vehicle, which then headed to Rom's restaurant in Sturbridge. On our way to Rom's, we went through an intersection at the bottom of West Street, and our driver had to swerve to prevent an oncoming car from crashing into us. Aunt Jean leaned into my broken arm, and I knew instantly that my arm had broken again. I started to have a lot of pain, and I said to Jean, "I think my arm just re-broke." She said, "Well, let's go to the hospital." I said, "No, I have to finish Mike's funeral. I'll go tomorrow morning." I knew I would be going back into surgery, and I wanted to be with my girls tonight.

We arrived at Rom's Restaurant. It could hold five hundred people, and the place was packed. There had been more than a thousand people at the mass. We had a buffet, and everything was very good, but I was in so much pain at that point that I just wanted it to be over so I could go home to my girls. I needed a hug from them so badly.

I arrived home later that afternoon, drained. I called the hospital to check on Kyle, and they said there had been no change. I had thought I would be able to go see him, but I was in so much pain that I couldn't. I called the nurse practitioner Mary Kay Seguin that I'd had in the hospital. She had given me her number just in case I needed anything. I called her to tell her I needed to be checked. I thought my arm was broken again, and I was having stomach pain. I thought I might have a hernia. She told me to page her when I arrived in the morning.

I sat down with the girls, and Kim asked me if I could read that special book I'd told them about. I said, "Sure." The book was about death, coffins, and the cemetery. I read the book to the girls and explained all the pictures as I went along. They asked some questions and handled it very well. They loved how Daddy had a pillow, and they thought he would be comfortable. I told them that Daddy had their ties on and looked so handsome, and they smiled. I said, "Daddy and Kyle love you both very much, and I am so proud of both of you. Thank you for being such wonderful little girls."

I woke up early the next morning, realizing that I might be going into surgery that day. I felt drained and was still very tired from Mike's wake and burial. I had breakfast with the girls and told them I needed to go see the doctor about my arm. I explained to the girls that I would have to stay at the hospital for a few days while the doctor fixed my arm, and that I needed to be with Kyle. I promised that I would call them and said they would be okay because everyone was helping to take care of them. The girls looked sad, but they understood that I needed to fix my arm, as they could see how swollen it was. I was upset that I had to leave them again. My life was just so hard and complicated, but there wasn't much I could do about it. I needed to go see Kyle and have my arm looked at.

Uncle Ronald brought me back to U-Mass Hospital, and I saw Mary Kay. She confirmed that I had broken my arm again and that I had a hernia. She said they would admit me and get me into surgery later that day as an add-on. I was so nervous but Mary Kay had this soft and tender way about her. She made me feel that everything would be okay. This time I had a different orthopedic doctor, Dr. Brian Busconi and I was worried that I could still lose my arm, but he assured me that he would do whatever he could—and that they would also fix my hernia.

I went upstairs to see Kyle. He was just lying there with tubes coming out of his mouth and nose. I could hear the machines running and the IV machine working. It had been eleven days now, and Kyle was still in critical condition. I wondered to myself, *how much can his little body take? Will he ever wake up?* I sat with Kyle for hours, holding his hand and praying for a miracle, trying to make sense of everything that had happened. I was still in shock that my husband had died, but I couldn't focus on losing Mike. I knew I had to be strong for my three children, and I was thinking of all the things I needed to do and all the promises I'd made to Mike. I was determined to follow through on each promise.

I sat with Kyle, telling him how much I loved him and that his sisters missed him very much. I told him he was in a hospital, that we had been in an accident, and that he had hurt his head very badly. I assured him that he was getting better every day and that he must keep fighting. I told him how much his father and I loved him. I had put on Daddy's CD, knowing how much Kyle loved his soft tender voice. Hearing Daddy's voice felt so good and soothing, but it instantly brought me to tears. Mike's music was soft and calming, but it made me realize how much I was missing him. As I wiped my tears, a nurse came in with a wheelchair and said it was time for me to go to pre-op for my surgery. I told Kyle, "I'll be back as soon as I can. Enjoy Daddy's music. I love you!"

My surgery went well. Dr. Busconi redid my arm, but this time the incision went to my shoulder. He had to put in more screws to hold the shattered bone, and he also pulled a nerve from my shoulder to regrow to my fingers. My hernia was fixed also. I was just so relieved that I still had my arm.

The pain was bad, but I was afraid to take strong meds because Kyle needed me, and I needed to be alert for him. I asked to go and see Kyle, but they said I needed to wait a little longer to let the anesthesia wear off. The only good thing about my needing surgery again was that I was close to Kyle. I could see him day and night, but I felt sad for my two little girls at home. I'd been discharged only one day ago, and now I was back in the hospital.

Chapter 11

Two weeks after the accident, Keith Doucette, age twenty-five, was arrested by state troopers upon his release from Saint Vincent's Hospital. They took him to Dudley District Court for arraignment on eleven charges, including vehicular homicide. Judge Philbin set bail at $10,000 cash. Keith had broken his leg in the accident. I could not be in court that day because my daughter and I were being released the same day—and I had Mike's wake that night.

When I heard that Judge Philbin had set bail at $10,000, I was in shock. How could that be? The man had a record of motor violations a mile long. How was it that my husband's and Kyle's lives were valued at only $10,000? He had killed my husband, and my son was in a coma. I wondered, *what kind of system do we have?*

Two months later, on December 24th, we had to go to court. This time I knew Keith would be in court. I was terrified, as I had no idea what to expect. I was shaking badly and couldn't hold back tears. I was afraid to come face-to-face with the man who had changed my life and taken so much from me. I was in terrible pain. My arm was in a cast, and I was bruised with hematomas all along the left sides of my legs. I still felt numb and weak. And I was still in shock. I couldn't believe that my son was in a coma and I didn't have my husband by my side. I had to be brave and go to court to see whom this man was, to see the person who had taken so much from me. I had my family with me, and my brother-in-law Norman explained what was going to happen in the courtroom.

A wonderful woman from the office came to the lobby and brought us to an office in the back room. She explained to me what was going to happen and tried to relax me, as I was shaking so much. She also shared information with me about car insurance. She told me that when there is a death in a car accident, like Mike's, the insurance company should pay for the funeral bill. There was also a victim fund available. She gave me papers to take home and read. I was surprised to hear all of this and was thankful that she had shared the information with me.

Then it was time to go into the courtroom. I was still shaking, scared to death, but my parents, Uncle Ronald and Gloria, Norman, and other family members were with me. I remember seeing Keith Doucette's family for the first time. I actually felt bad for them, because I knew it must have been hard to accept what their son had done. There was so much hurt and tears, and none of us knew what was going to happen. I had no idea what Keith looked like. Was he tall, short, stocky, or skinny? Did he have brown or black hair? Would he even care about what had happened? Would he be crying? Did he even realize what he had done? I had so many questions in my mind, but I realized that many of them would never be answered.

Keith came into the courtroom on crutches. He was tall and thin, had light-brown hair, and was dressed in a blue suit. Before the hearing began, I left the courtroom through a side door. Walking not more than three feet from him, I stared at him. I wanted a good look. I needed to see his eyes.

Keith looked down at the floor. It seemed to me that he didn't have any emotion, and that made me angry and hurt. I wanted to say, "Don't you even know what you did, what you took from me? You killed my husband. My ten-year-old son is in a coma, and we don't know if he will live or die. My girls and I were badly injured." But I couldn't say anything. I had to sit there and listen to the judge and the district attorney.

Keith Doucette was arraigned on eleven charges. Among them was vehicular homicide while driving under the influence of alcohol with negligence, four counts of drunken driving causing serious bodily injury with negligence, two marked lanes violations, negligent driving, speeding, a passing violation, and a tire-tread depth violation. He pleaded not guilty to all the charges. Judge Austin Philbin set bail at $10,000 cash.

The Registry of Motor Vehicles had decided to revoke his license three days prior to our accident, to be suspended on November 8th for thirty days. He'd had three speeding violations in one year, among the seventeen driving offenses on his RMV record.

I was shocked. I couldn't believe that the person who had destroyed my family was someone with such a long record. I knew he was someone who didn't care, and feeling that way made me angrier. I wanted him to be remorseful, to show some feelings, but instead he was stone-faced. I just couldn't understand how someone could be that way. I left the courtroom unhappy. I couldn't believe he'd gotten bail and pleaded not guilty. I knew that lots of people did so, but he'd had alcohol and drugs in his system. To me, "not guilty" was a big joke.

Chapter 12

Two months had passed, and I needed to take care of some bills from Mike's funeral. I went to my vehicle insurance company and asked my agent about the information the women at the courthouse had given me about my car insurance helping to pay for Mike's funeral expenses because of the way he'd died. My agent looked it up and said the information was correct. It was something they had not been aware of, and they were surprised. I gave the insurance company Mike's funeral bill, and they submitted a payment to Sansoucy's Funeral Home.

The woman in the courthouse had also informed me about the victim's fund. When someone dies in an accident, the survivors are entitled to a sum of money, and each person in the accident can receive a refund for any medical costs that are not covered. I got to use this fund for my medical expenses. Because I couldn't work any longer, I got to collect my wages. Kyle's money was used for some medical equipment that wasn't covered by insurance. I never got to use the girls' money, but it was a great help and a relief to know that this program was there. I don't think I would ever have known about the fund if it hadn't been for the wonderful woman at the courthouse.

I started to look for a gravestone for Mike. I didn't want to put it off, because I knew I wanted something very special and different. Uncle Ronald went with me to several places, and we fell in love with a six-foot, mauve-colored stone. It was a different shape from the other stones, and we put planters on each side. Pepin Granite gave us ideas for decorating the stone, and we started with flowers and a cross at the top. I put a little-boy angel representing Kyle on one side and the Virgin Mary in the middle. On the other side of Mary, I put a little-girl angel to represent Kimberly and Katie, and at the bottom was our last name: Brodeur. The front of the stone turned out amazing. The back of the stone said:

"It doesn't matter where you go or what you
do. It is who you have beside you."

[oval picture of us]

In loving memory of my best friend, husband, and father.
Words cannot express our emptiness without you.
You will always be in our hearts forever, and we
will cherish you always until we meet again.

Michael David Brodeur 9/10/59-1/1/97

Lisa Ann Matte 9/9/67-

When it was all drawn up, I was very excited. It was gorgeous. I had ordered my dream stone. I wanted Mike to have the very best, something different that I hadn't seen before, and Uncle Ronald and I had accomplished that. It felt so good to be able to do something for my wonderful husband.

The stone was delivered in late spring, and it was just gorgeous. I remember being so excited to put flowers in the planters. I was with Kyle so much at Spaulding Rehab that I couldn't get to the store right away to purchase flowers, but a coworker and friend, Rene Ferron, got flowers and put them in to surprise me. When I finally arrived at the cemetery and saw the flowers, I cried. They were so beautiful! I will never forget what that meant to me.

The front of Michael's gravestone, designed by Lisa. The boy angel represents Kyle, and tthe girl angel represents Kimberly and Katie.

The back of Michael's gravestone

Chapter 13

It was another day, but this one was a little different. Mike's CD had just finished playing, and when it stopped, Kyle's heart monitor went off. I thought it was a coincidence. Martha, Kyle's nurse came in and said that his heart rate had just gone up but that he was okay now.

I started to talk to Kyle, and all of a sudden the monitor went off again. Again, Martha said it was nothing. I waited a bit before talking again, and the same thing happened. I said, "He knows I'm here!" Martha said he was too heavily sedated, that he couldn't know. I believed that Kyle knew I was there. I put his daddy's music back on, told him how much I loved him, and said I would always be there for him.

After nearly a month, Kyle had undergone several surgeries. He had started to take some breaths on his own, but we were nowhere near to removing the breathing tube. His eyes had opened, and we were reducing his meds slowly to what he could handle. To me, these were big improvements. The doctor still believed that Kyle was going to be a vegetable, but I felt different. Why would the heart monitor always go off when Mike's CD ended? Why, when I went in to talk to him, did the monitor go off? To me it was a sign that Kyle was there. He just needed time to heal. I prayed and prayed and felt like God was answering my prayers.

I noticed marks on Kyle from having so much blood drawn. I asked Martha if they could hold off and give him a break for a day or so. She said okay, if that was what I wanted. The next day, I arrived, and Kyle's eyes were open. I was so happy, but his eyes were different, discolored. I pressed the call button for Martha to come in, and I said, "Something is wrong. I don't like the way his eyes look. Can you do a blood test?" She said, "I thought you wanted a break." I said I felt that something was wrong. Martha took blood from Kyle, and the test came back showing that his liver function was off, so meds were given to fix the problem.

Each week we were seeing improvements. To me, they were huge steps. Kyle was starting to take more breaths on his own, and we weren't being rushed into surgeries as we had been during the first two weeks. There were no seizures or heavy breathing.

U-Mass provided us a financial councilor Cathy Conway, she provided me information on disability since I could no longer work, and suggested Kyle apply for Massachusetts health insurance since his medical expenses were so outrageous. She was a blessing and willing to help any way she could. A representative from Spaulding Rehab, Linda Hamlin came to visit us, she was a great help. Linda suggested that we needed to start thinking about rehab for Kyle. I said, "How can he go to rehab in a coma?" She said, "When Kyle is off the ventilator and is holding his own, he will be ready, and hopefully he will come out of his coma."

I asked for her suggestions, and she said there were two facilities in Boston that would meet Kyle's needs. Linda gave me their names, and I went to visit each of them. I decided I wanted to put Kyle at Spaulding Rehab. I was terrified of leaving U-Mass, but I was thankful I still had Kyle, and I knew it would take a very long time for him to recover.

After four weeks, it was our first holiday, Thanksgiving. Waking up that morning, I wondered how I could be thankful. I had lost the love of my life. My son was still in a coma, not breathing on his own, and I still didn't know if he would survive or not. My girls were coping, but they were having a hard time. Katie was not too happy about her body cast, and Kim was struggling with her speech. The girls missed their father and brother, and I couldn't be home a lot to take care of them.

Life was a struggle, but I had to be thankful! In order to get through this day, I knew I had to stop thinking about what I didn't have and focus on what I did have. I had my two beautiful daughters alive, and I knew they would heal physically, although emotionally it would take a long time. My son was still alive, and I was there to take care of my family. At least they still had one parent. I also had good family and friends and much love in my life. I tried to focus on that.

I made the girls breakfast, and later on we had Thanksgiving next door with Meme Rita, Mike's family, and some of my family. We all sat down to eat, and everything looked wonderful, as usual. Katie was put in a chair, fitting awkwardly because of her body cast, but she did fine. Kimberly sat beside me. My sister Laurie said grace, saying how thankful she was to have all of us with her today. She said how much she wished Mike and Kyle were with us and how very loved they both were. Everyone was in tears. It was very difficult for all of us, but we had each other to help us get through the day.

After the meal, Uncle Ronald and I went to visit Kyle. He was still in a deep sleep, and the nurse said he had been pretty much the same all day. We stayed for an hour or so, but we were so exhausted, we went home. I wanted to try to spend some time with my girls.

The girls were being spoiled, as everyone was constantly buying them things. Katie was very demanding, ordering everyone around, and she acted out a lot. Kim was trying to adjust to being back at school, and it was difficult because of her speech. Kim had an evaluation and received speech therapy for a while. It was an anxiety issue, and it would take a very long time for her to heal. The girls were happy to have me home with them.

After seven weeks, Kyle was still showing little progress. I was in his room, just talking to him about his sisters and what was happening. I was holding his hand, when suddenly his hand clenched mine. Oh my God, Kyle had held my hand! I immediately called the nurse, but again she thought it was just a coincidence. I waited a little while and then put my hand back in his—and the same thing happened. I said, "I'm sorry, but this isn't a coincidence. He knows I'm here."

The nurse put her hand in Kyle's and said; "Kyle, if you hear me, squeeze my hand," but Kyle did nothing. Later on, I held his hand again, and he squeezed it again. This went on for weeks, but he would only hold my hand. This gave me so much hope. My little boy was in there somewhere.

Then came the big day when Kyle came off the ventilator. He was breathing on his own! He still had the feeding line in his nose, but his stomach was healed, his eyes were open, and he still squeezed my hand—and when his father's CD stopped, his monitors would go off. To me, it was wonderful, and I was excited.

A physical therapist came in to examine Kyle, and we noticed that he was getting tight muscle tone. She removed the sheets to exercise his legs. I couldn't believe what I saw: his feet were turned inward. In shock, I asked, "When did this happen? How come no one said anything about this?" She said this was her first time with Kyle, and she didn't know.

I asked the doctor about it, and he said they were so busy keeping Kyle alive that they had only been concerned with everything from his stomach up. It wasn't his department to worry about Kyle's feet, and he expected that rehab would work on them. I knew we would be heading to Spaulding, and that was something they would work on there. I couldn't be angry, because I knew Kyle had kept them very busy with so many ups and downs. They were wonderful people, and most importantly, Kyle was alive!

I went to kiss Kyle good-bye, and he tried to move his lips. He just looked at me, and it gave me so much hope!

Chapter 14

Christmas was two weeks away, and I knew I had to celebrate it for the girls' sake. My father went with me to get a tree, and we put it up next to the hospital beds in the living room. Kim was a huge help. We put Katie in a chair and gave her ornaments to put on, which was very hard for her. The girls were very happy to have a tree, but it was very different, not having their father and Kyle with us. I had to put up a good front for the girls, but deep down, I was dying inside. It didn't feel like Christmas. It was a very hard time for me, but I knew I had to do it for my girls.

I asked Aunt Jean if I could leave, as I needed some fresh air. I took a walk by myself by the Rez in Southbridge to clear my head. I had so much anger in me that I started crying and throwing rocks. I missed my husband and son so much. In my eyes, I'd had the perfect little family, and I had been so happy. How could this be happening? I knew I couldn't change things, but I wished so badly that I could.

When I got back home, I drove my car to the cemetery. I needed to be with Mike. I sat on the ground, just filling him in on everything that was happening. I promised him that I would be strong and wouldn't let the kids see all my pain. I needed strength more than anything. There was so much ahead of me with all the decisions about Kyle. It was overwhelming. I promised Mike that I would always go with my gut feelings on decisions. So far, I thought I was doing well. I asked Mike, "Why did you have to die? Why didn't I die? Sometimes I wished it had been me that had died, because life was just too much to handle at times. I knew I had to accept that he was gone and I had survived, but it didn't make it easier.

After visiting Kyle one night, I stopped at Toys"R"Us to do Christmas shopping. I didn't really want to be there, but I needed some toys for the girls. Going through the aisles, I saw husbands and wives shopping together, and it brought me to tears. I envied them and wanted my husband. Mike and I had done everything together, and it was a new experience for me going shopping alone. I saw so many things that I normally would have gotten for Kyle, but I knew he couldn't do the sports stuff any longer. He didn't even know anything at this stage.

I was crying as I threw dolls and toys in my carriage, and people were staring at me, not knowing what I was going through. I just needed to finish and get out of there. At that point, I was still in a lot of physical pain, as my legs, back, and arm were still trying to heal. Emotionally, I did the best I could, but I had some really difficult times, especially when I was by myself. During those times when I was alone, I could release my anger and hurt. I didn't have to be strong, because my kids weren't with me.

The girls received a visit from Mr. and Mrs. Santa Claus (Bill and Celeste Rivernider). They were so wonderful to think of my girls. Santa asked the girls what they wanted for Christmas, and they recited their lists. Katie was very talkative. Kimberly was a little shy before warming up, and she had trouble speaking. They sang some Christmas songs and talked about their daddy and Kyle. It was a wonderful surprise visit that made the girls very happy.

We also had a visit from Clarity the Clown. She brought a rabbit with her, which the kids loved, and she did some magic tricks and face painting. It was so nice to see the girls smile and be happy.

The Dudley Courthouse and area law enforcement donated toys, stuffed animals, dolls, food, and money. I was shocked when they brought it all to my house. Our accident had touched so many people, and everyone just wanted to help in any way they could. It really touched me to know that so many people cared about our family and that they haven't forgotten us. The girls went crazy, picking out whatever they wanted, as there was so much!

The night before Christmas, we put out cookies and milk for Santa. And we had another tradition: watching Santa put the presents under the tree. Uncle Ronald was Santa, and he always made it interesting for the kids. He always did something silly to make them laugh. My sister Linda and her family stayed with us for Christmas, and all our kids hid quietly on the stairs. I stayed with Katie in her hospital bed and covered us with a blanket. We all knew we needed to be really quiet, because if Santa knew we were awake, he wouldn't leave us presents.

Santa came into the room multiple times, placing presents under our tree and bending over and having gas. The kids just loved that. I always left the kids' pictures out, and Santa always kissed them. Then he drank his milk and had some cookies, made loud noises, and cleared his throat. When he was done, he rang his bells, and the kids ran to bed. They knew that if Santa flew over the house and they were awake, he would take the presents back.

On Christmas morning, the kids were excited. Linda's family was with us, and Meme Rita, Aunt Jean and Lucien, and Ronald and Gloria came over. We had a full house, which made it so nice for the kids. For me, it was very hard, as I was missing Mike and Kyle, but I tried hard to be happy for the girls. The girls enjoyed their presents, and we all had dinner together. Overall, it was a nice day. I went to visit Kyle at night and brought him a big stuffed bear. He had no clue that it was Christmas day.

Tomorrow was a big day. Kyle was being discharged from U-Mass Hospital and were going to Spaulding Rehab in Boston. I was excited and nervous, but I was thinking positive thoughts. It was going to be hard to say good-bye to the doctors and nurses in whom I had put so much trust. I was so thankful for everyone at U-Mass Hospital. They had taken really good care of my whole family. U-Mass had been my home for two months. I hoped the people at Spaulding would be just as nice—but more importantly that they would be able to help my son with his recovery.

When I returned to U-Mass for my last time, Kyle was still in his coma, but there were no machines breathing for him. He still had a feeding tube in his nose. Martha disconnected the monitors so I could put clothes on him for the first time in two months. Kyle was dressed in his hockey shirt, comfy stretch pants, and socks. He could no longer wear sneakers, as his feet were all deformed. I was so happy to be going to a rehab center. This was huge progress. My son was alive and no longer needed breathing machines! I could only hope for more progress in time.

It was sad, saying good-bye to everyone, especially Martha and Dr. Wood. Through my two months dealing with Dr. Wood, I valued his opinion, his kindness, and his support. I was so thankful for all the doctors and nurses and my case manager. The ambulance arrived, and we took pictures, gave lots of hugs, and shed many tears when we left. We were off on our next adventure!

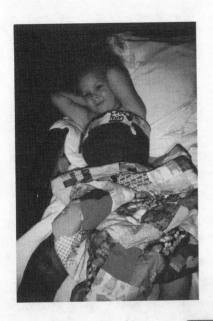

Katie, three years old, in her body cast for 8 weeks with a broken femur, 1997

Kim and Katie back home, Santa Clause came to visit before Christmas, 1997.

Chapter 15

It was a cold day as I arrived at Spaulding Rehab. I was very nervous and waited anxiously to meet the new doctors and therapist for Kyle. The paramedics brought Kyle to the pediatric floor. Stepping out of the elevator, I noticed therapy rooms, offices, and a lunchroom. Going through a set of doors, I noticed all the young patients in their rooms, parents by their sides, looking at Kyle and me.

When we arrived at Kyle's room, the paramedics put Kyle in his new bed. We had a roommate, a young man around Kyle's age. A friendly and sweet nurse named Kathy came in and took Kyle's history. Then we met Kyle's new doctor, Dr. Susan Rosenberg. She seemed very young but very smart. We discussed a brief summary of Kyle, and that he had also had two strokes at the scene of the accident. The doctor was going to do a physical examination, and then we would make a plan for his recovery and set some goals. Kyle would have occupational, physical, and speech therapies while he was there.

After the doctor evaluated Kyle, she talked to me about his coma, explaining that there were many stages to a coma and that Kyle was in the second stage of the Glasgow coma scale. Every week a test would be given to him. Using a chart, the doctor would follow Kyle's test points to determine his current coma stage. The tests would include his eyes and verbal and motor skills. According to the Ranchos Los Amigos Scale, Kyle was presently in the vegetative state.

Kyle would also be going to Children's Hospital to be evaluated by a neurologist. Tomorrow he would meet with his therapist, who would set up a plan and decide how many times per week to see Kyle. This was a lot of information for one day, and I was overwhelmed.

Kyle's therapists came in separately throughout the day, and they were all pleasant and very nice. Donna, a physical therapist, came in and said she would be working with Kyle. We went over his history, and when she moved his limbs, she noticed that his muscle tone was very tight. I mentioned that his feet were twisted as well. She said it was a result of the brain injury and that his muscle tone was so severe that it was putting Kyle in spasms that deformed his feet.

Donna recommended that we do serial casting to see if we could gradually correct his feet. If we couldn't, a surgical procedure would be required. So far, his spine was okay, but she was worried about his muscle tone affecting his spine. Donna recommended that we go to an orthopedist at Children's Hospital.

Michelle, the occupational therapist, came in, and she was very sweet also. Michelle evaluated Kyle and noticed that his right hand was tight, while his left side was loose. She recommended putting a cast on Kyle's right arm to see if we could break his muscle tone. I thought this was very interesting. By casting, we were trying to reteach the brain to not allow the muscle tone to be in his arm.

Lynette, the speech therapist, was also kind and sweet. When she came in and evaluated Kyle, she said that she would start by trying to get him to respond to things like a cold towel, swabbing his lips, toys, and so on.

I found it all very interesting, but I also realized that we had a lot of therapy and work ahead of us. And Kyle would need a lot of casting. I just hoped he could handle it all.

It was Katie's birthday. She was four years old, and she was getting her body cast removed. What a birthday present! Uncle Ronald and Aunt Gloria brought us to U-Mass. Katie was in a wheelchair, excited but afraid. A wonderful, kind man lifted Katie to a table. He took out his electric saw and put it on his own hand to show her that it didn't hurt. She giggled, reassured that she would feel no pain, just a little vibration.

The technician turned on his saw and started to cut her cast open. Her big, blue eyes got huge, and I held her hand, praising her. Before we knew it, she was released from a cast that had encased her for two long months. Her skin was chafed, so we rubbed her with body lotion. After two long months, we could finally put clothes on her. I was so excited!

Katie was petrified, and she cried. All she had known was that cast. She was afraid to bear her own weight, and she wouldn't even put her feet on the ground. She screamed in fear. The therapist suggested using a little walker to help her until she felt comfortable, but Katie wanted nothing to do with it. She wanted us to carry her everywhere. It was really hard, because I needed her to relearn how to walk.

One afternoon at home, Katie was playing on the floor. She wanted a drink, and I told her she had to get up and get it. She refused, screaming. It had been a few days since the cast had been removed, and the doctor said I couldn't baby her. She needed to get those muscles going again. She was getting physical therapy, and they said she was fine to walk, but she was scared. So I had to let her cry as I explained that she could walk.

When she saw that I wasn't going to give in to her, she got up and started to use her walker. I was so proud of her, but boy did she make me shake. It took a week or two for her to feel safe, and then she was off and running. I told her she could plan her birthday party, now that she was walking. She said she wanted a pool party.

What a great week! Kyle was off to Spaulding, and I was excited about all the new things we would be trying with him. And Katie's body cast had been removed. Slowly but surely, things were coming together. Before I knew it, Katie would be able to go back to preschool.

Chapter 16

Bill LaPoint, a man I had never met, read about what had happened to our family, and he decided he wanted to do a fundraiser in the Grand Ball Room at the Sturbridge Host Hotel. Cactus, a four-time "Band of the Year," with a special appearance by Jay Beaupre of Panning for Gold and the DJ services of Mike Soulor of Q100 Atlanta radio provided entertainment. Approximately 750 people attended. The night was filled with love, and everyone had a great time. The girls attended in matching outfits and patent leather shoes. They loved having their pictures taken and tried to dance to the country music.

Norman, my brother-in-law, gave a speech. He said that this accident had turned him into a better person. Seeing accidents and suffering on the job used to be routine business for him, but now he saw things differently. "I'm a better officer because of this," he said.

The huge outpouring of support stunned me for the girls and myself. I attempted a short speech, but tears got in the way when I tried to say that my husband would have been proud. It was so difficult. I had so much emotion going on. I kept thinking of Kyle and what he was missing.

We had a good time, and I was very thankful to Bill LaPoint for giving us a night that I will never forget.

Later that week, there was a letter in the newspaper that said: "Say a prayer for Kyle. I'd like to ask that we come together as a community and pray for a little child. We should ask God to heal Kyle Brodeur.

There is much power in prayer, and nothing is impossible with the Lord. Kyle Brodeur needs our prayers, and the Lord will touch and heal him. He will remove him from the coma and allow him to face whatever he can remember. Please pray for his mother's safety, as she travels into Worcester to see her son every day. Pray that God will heal her and her two daughters. Take a moment each day to ask God to touch Kyle and his family." The letter was signed: "One who cares, Southbridge."

I loved this letter so much. I didn't know who wrote it, but I cried when I read it. I can't tell you what it meant to me as a mother, knowing those months after our accident, people were still thinking about my family and me and trusting in the power of prayer.

While Kyle was at U-Mass in a coma, the Worcester Ice Cats hockey team came to visit. As part of the community outreach program, they stopped regularly in the pediatric ward. Kyle was not aware of anything then. I felt horrible, because Kyle and his dad had often gone to their games, and I knew Kyle would have been thrilled to see them and get an autograph. Since Kyle loved the Ice Cats, Madden handed me his business card with his phone number and said, "When he gets better, give us a call, and we'll have him be a guest at a game." I was so happy, thinking, *Kyle, you need to wake up! You are going to love meeting the Ice Cats!* I said good-bye and told Madden I would be in touch.

Almost a year later, I called Madden, and he remembered us. We set up a time to arrive early before a game so that Kyle could meet the players. My girls and I went too. On the way to practice, the players shook gloves with Kyle. His blue eyes opened wide, and he moved his right hand to shake theirs. He had so much to say, but he couldn't get the words out of his mouth. But his facial expression said it all. He was clearly happy and full of excitement. The captain gave Kyle an autographed stick, a T-shirt, and a pennant. Kyle's eyes filled with tears. During the game, Madden announced that Kyle was a guest of honor. It was a night that Kyle would never forget.

Another special night occurred at a Southbridge High basketball game. A group called Kids for Kyle put on a fundraiser, raffling off two football cards at halftime. A woman named Marge Schwall and her son Cory had met us at a sports card show that was being done in Kyle's honor by Mr. Veshia and LJ Sports cards. Cory had left the card show feeling that he wanted to do something for Kyle, so they had organized the Kids for Kyle group. During halftime at the Southbridge basketball game, Kyle's name was announced, and he received a standing ovation. Cory pushed Kyle's wheelchair—with Kyle's sisters and friends following—to the announcer to pull the raffle ticket. It was a very emotional event with lots of tears. People were seeing Kyle for the first time in a cast up to his thighs, realizing that this was Kyle's tenth surgery in just fifteen months.

The song "Hero," sung by Renee Mungeon, was dedicated to Kyle for his strength and courage. It was amazing. Kyle looked at her in awe, his eyes glossy with excitement. After the song, there was another standing ovation, and we went back to our seats. What a night! We felt blessed to be so loved.

Every year for ten years, there was a golf tournament in memory of Michael. The Langevin brother's started this event then it was taken over by Mike's family. We were so fortunate to participate in this event. It was a day my children and I could attend, and we saw so many people that Mike had been friendly with. It was a hard day for me, seeing all the guys and thinking that Mike should have been there with them, playing and having fun. Instead, it was a day of memories for me, as I felt robbed by something that shouldn't have happened. But I had to adjust to the reality of my husband never coming back.

Even though it was hard, I was very thankful. The tournament day was always a great success, and we were able to give scholarships out every year in Mike's memory. The best part for my children was getting T-shirts with their daddy's name on them. They wore them to bed every night. Seeing so many people who cared was also good for the kids. They knew that their father was loved and had been a very special person to many people.

Every year, my children and I presented a scholarship in memory of their father, Michael Brodeur, which was difficult for me. I was always shaking and tearful as I read about what a wonderful man Mike had been and how a drunk driver had cut his life short. As my girls got older, I wanted them to take over for me. Kimberly was too bashful, but Katie said she would do it, and she did. I was so proud, listening to her and thinking how proud her daddy would have been. She was only ten years old and was talking in front of a couple hundred people. Then Kyle and Kimberly would hand out the scholarship. The arrangement worked out well and was a big relief for me.

Chapter 17

Three to five times a week, I went to U-Mass Hospital for my own occupational or physical therapy. These sessions were very painful for my arm. After nearly three months of healing, my arm showed little progress and no movement. The therapists were doing easy stretches to my upper arm, the pain of which about killed me. They tried to stretch each of my fingers. I had a removable cast to wear every day. Elastic bands held my fingers up, and a pin in my thumb had recently come out. The pin helped to heal the bone, because my thumb had come off in the accident. The therapist tried to keep me from getting discouraged, telling me it was going to take a full year. I had to be patient and wait for the nerve to regrow from my shoulder to my fingers. I had to limit the therapy I did on my own, because it was possible to over-exercise the arm.

I was adjusting to having one arm, but I still needed a lot of help, especially to do my hair, put on my bra and shirt, and tie my shoes. I wasn't doing much cooking, as I was hardly home. My schedule was crazy. I would go to therapy almost every day and then head to Boston to see Kyle. I stayed with Kyle at Spaulding until nighttime, got my ride home, and saw the girls for an hour or so before bedtime. Then I woke up in the morning and did it all over again, still depending on my family to help out with the girls during the day until I came home.

I was with Kyle on Monday through Friday. On the weekends, my parents went to be with him, and if they couldn't go, my sister Gina or

Mike's niece Michelle went. I needed to have some time with my girls. They really missed me and were acting out over it. They loved it when I took them to visit Kyle. They would hop right in bed with him, and Kyle would just stare at them while they giggled. Katie and Kim would say, "Kyle, talk to me," and I would have to explain that Kyle couldn't talk right now but that he was listening. I had them practice colors, shapes, and the alphabet with him.

Kyle loved to see family photos. We were trying to show him things that were familiar to him. The girls sang a lot Barney songs and recited nursery rhymes, as I needed to see if Kyle would react to anything. The girls loved it and felt like they were doing something good for him. At this stage, Kyle did a lot of staring, but I knew he was aware of what we were doing. The doctors and therapist told us that coming out of a coma were like starting from stage one again as a baby, relearning everything. I figured that if we did easy stuff with him, maybe I would get a reaction and see what level he was at.

At this stage, we dressed Kyle every day and put him in a wheelchair so he could get out of bed. I wheeled him around the halls and took him outside by the water to see the ducks. It was nice just to have some fresh air. We ordered a special wheelchair just for Kyle. It was measured to fit his body and was designed with the special laterals, seat cushions, leg rest, and headrest he needed.

Kyle's body was changing every day, and we noticed that his muscle tone was getting worse. The physical therapist put casts on his legs, trying to break his muscle tone. Kyle didn't do very well with it, as he was having many spasms. He actually started to holler out in pain. The sweating was unbelievable, and it only got worse. He would soak through his bedding in no time. I felt like all I did was give him cold towels. We had to remove the cast. Dr. Rosenberg suggested trying some Botox to see if it could help his muscle tone, but it didn't touch him. We made an appointment to see a pain specialist at Children's Hospital.

Kyle's first appointment for the day was with his neurologist Dr. Basil Darras. He was very nice and pleasant and easy to talk to. Going over Kyle's medical history, he was amazed that Kyle had even survived.

The doctor explained that comas can take a very long time to come out of, and sometimes a person might never come out. He said that time would tell us everything. He suggested that we should be happy at this point with any signs he gave us and that I should keep doing what I was doing. The doctor thought Kyle's meds were good. We made another appointment and hoped we would see more progress.

On the orthopedic floor, we met with Dr. Fred Shapiro and discussed Kyle's feet. He took X-rays and decided that surgery was necessary. We decided to wait it out so that Kyle had a chance to recover more. I liked this doctor. He was very knowledgeable. We made an appointment to stay in touch.

Next in the pain clinic, we met Dr. Charles Berde, he had a lot of knowledge about Baclofen pumps. We talked about Kyle's brain injury and the fact that his meds by IV weren't working. Kyle's spasms were in his feet and neck, and Dr. Berde suggested a Baclofen pump. The pump is a size of a hockey puck; it would be inserted into his stomach and attached to his spinal cord by a catheter. He explained this would allow a constant feed of medicine at a small rate, which he hoped would help with the spasms. If we decided to do this, we would do a trial surgery first, stay for a few days to see how Kyle handled it, and see if there were any changes in his spasms. If it worked out, they would do another surgery and put in the permanent pump. Every few months we would come in for a procedure to refill the pump with Baclofen. It all sounded amazing to me, as I had never heard of it, but I knew we had to try it because his muscle tone was increasing rapidly.

Returning back to Spaulding we noticed Kyle's roommate was discharged, which meant that there was an empty bed in Kyle's room. I asked if I could sleep in it until they had another patient. Luckily, they said yes. They knew I was there day and night and that I traveled a little over an hour each way. It worked out well, because I didn't have to bother Uncle Ronald and other family and friends to bring me to U-Mass and then to Spaulding. The down side was that I wouldn't be going home every night to see my daughters.

The rides back and forth were killing me, and they were hard on my family members. I would go to Spaulding on a Monday morning and return home Friday night. My mom would then replace me to stay overnight with Kyle and then go home on Saturday or Sunday—to be replaced by someone else. Kyle was never left alone. We set up my own OT and PT appointments at Spaulding. With everything being done in one place, it made my life so much easier.

Kyle went to physical therapy a few times each week. He always put his right finger in his mouth, which became a bad, impulsive habit. I knew he recognized me, and I also knew he could follow some directions. At that time, he still had his feeding line in his nose. Donna, his physical therapist, decided to put Kyle on a big exercise ball, as we were trying to wake him up and get him to have a reaction. Well, it worked. He hated it and cried out. We tried to make him stay on the ball for as long as he could tolerate it. It was awful to hear him cry out, but it was so nice that he was responding.

Kyle made some progress with speech. Lynette put some garlic near Kyle's nose, and he clearly didn't like the smell—, which was big news, because we knew his senses were working. It was very difficult for Kyle to stay awake at this stage. It seemed that every time we went to speech therapy, Kyle was very sleepy. We consistently used a cold towel to wake him up. We even tried to change the time of day that he went, but it didn't seem to matter much.

Michelle, his occupational therapist, elicited some progress also. She taught Kyle how to do "thumbs up" for yes and "thumbs down" for no. This was a huge development, because it was a good way to communicate with him. We knew at this stage that he knew us, but we still received nothing verbal. He was very sleepy, and his muscle tone was still increasing.

Chapter 18

Sitting by Kyle's bedside and watching him sleep so peacefully; I couldn't help but think of everything he and I had endured since he was born.

The day that changed my life forever was the day that Kyle was born: July 23, 1987. He was a huge baby, weighing eight pounds and thirteen ounces. The nurse placed Kyle in my arms. He was so sweet and handsome, and he had so many little rolls of baby fat. I just couldn't believe that he was mine. He was such a good baby. His father, who was also named Kyle, was in his glory. He had a son. He had even worn blue that day, hoping he would have a boy.

Kyle Sr. and I had dated for two years and then decided to marry in 1985. I was eighteen and Kyle was twenty. Life with Kyle was hard at times, and being so young, especially financially. We did the best we could with what little funds we had. Our biggest enjoyment was our baby boy. We were both in love with him. I had a full-time job at Commerce Insurance, and Kyle worked at Flexcon. I enjoyed my time off with my baby so much that when it came time to leave him and return to work, I just couldn't. Kyle and I figured out that paying for a sitter would have taken half my pay. We decided that I would quit Commerce and apply for a part-time job at Harrington Memorial Hospital. Luckily, I was hired in the admissions office, and I loved my job. I worked second shift three days a week and every other weekend. Our baby went to a sitter for only six to nine hours a week until Kyle Sr. picked him up.

On my husband's birthday, he turned the big twenty-one, and we had a nice little party with his family. It had been a tough few years there after, and we were both growing in different directions. We had different family values, and over time it made us drift apart even more. I was no longer happy, and our marriage of only three years came to an end.

I never went back to Kyle Sr. I had to take control of my own life. I had to find a full-time job, so I went back to Commerce Insurance. I put Kyle in the daycare there. It was convenient, and I could even see him at lunchtime. I thought everything would work out, but little Kyle didn't like the separation. He got really sick, with vomiting and high blood pressure. He was not the same little boy I'd always had.

I brought him to his pediatrician Dr. Robert Giordano, who said that Kyle was struggling with the changes that had just taken place in his life. He recommended keeping Kyle out of daycare for a couple of weeks to get him happy and healthy again. That meant I had to quit my job. It took a month for Kyle to become the happy baby he had been. Now I was faced with unemployment. How was I going to support us? I had to pay for rent, a car payment, insurance, utilities, and food. Kyle Sr. would not give me child support on a weekly basis, since there wasn't a court order yet.

I hired an attorney to start divorce proceedings and to get child support. I started searching for a job right away. I took a job at United Lens Company in Southbridge. It was a full-time job, and I was excited because I lived right down the road from it. My sister Laurie said she would babysit Kyle for me. I went to get help with daycare through Kids Unlimited, and it helped me a great deal.

My son would arrive at my sister's house around 7:15 a.m., and he just loved her. He still didn't like me leaving, but with my sister consoling him and giving him that special time, he did well over time. Kyle was always happy when I picked him up at 5:20 p.m., and I got the biggest hugs and kisses from him.

Kyle was always full of laughter and love, and we were very close. It was a struggle to survive and to make us a good home, but we did it, and I was so proud of what we accomplished together. Raising Kyle was my number-one priority, and I did everything I could to have him grow up in the best environment I could provide.

Looking at Kyle at ten years of age, lying there in a coma, I wanted those hugs and kisses more than anything in the world. He had always been his mommy's little boy, and I wanted that little boy back so badly. I wondered if I would ever get him back.

Kyle was starting to wake up. He couldn't move, but his eyes were open. I said, "Did you have a nice dream? You look so peaceful." I called the nurse in to reposition him. Kyle looked good overall, and his hair was starting to grow back. At that time, he still had the feeding line in his nose, and we didn't know if he would ever eat again. But I still had hope.

I was standing by Kyle's bedside, and his big, blue eyes were staring at me, watching me eat some ice chips. I started to feel bad, thinking that his mouth must be dry and that he might want some. I knew I wasn't supposed to give Kyle anything by mouth for fear that he would choke. I reasoned that it was just a little chip of ice; it would melt so fast that there was no way he could choke.

I sat Kyle up and put a piece of ice in his mouth. I was amazed at what I saw. He loved it! He started to move his tongue, and I put two pieces in this time. Again, he loved it. When I gave him a little more and he tried to chew it, I knew my little boy was going to eat. I immediately called for the nurse and told her what had happened. She couldn't believe that I'd done it without someone there to monitor it. We paged Kyle's speech therapist Lynette, and I showed her. She said, "Great! We will try soft food and see what happens."

Going to speech therapy that day was exciting. We gave Kyle more ice chips and even tried some pudding. Kyle had a ways to go, but throughout the day, I just kept giving him pudding and ice chips. Eventually, he became a little stronger, and it got easier to feed him. It took a long time to feed him the pudding, but at least he finished it. After a couple of weeks, we tried thickened liquids. Kyle couldn't use a straw, so I gave him a special cup. This was very exciting, but it was also time-consuming. It was a good thing I stayed with him five days a week, because I was able to practice his eating and do mouth exercises with him on a daily basis. Kyle was still very sleepy, as his therapy drained him. Together we put in a very busy day.

We needed to adapt the headrest in Kyle's wheelchair. He couldn't keep his head up, which made it hard for me to feed him. My arm was still in a sling, and I didn't have the use of it. We decided to try a headrest, but Kyle's muscle tone was getting worse and kept pulling him to the left side. We decided to attach a foam block to his headrest, hoping to keep his head centered for swallowing. We used a head strap to keep his head up. It helped but was still very challenging. His muscle tone was just too tough to break, and at times even the strap wouldn't stay. It was a miracle that I got food into him. He was a challenge, but I knew I couldn't give up. My mom and Aunt Jean made all of Kyle's food. They pureed everything. My sister Patty made my meals for the day and always made sure I had a good snack. Kyle and I were so lucky that my family helped out in this way. They made sure we were eating healthy. Kyle and I always enjoyed our mealtimes. They were our favorite times of day!

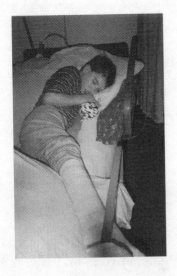

Kyle, in a comatose state after four months, 1998. A ball was used as part of therapy to try to keep his hand open.

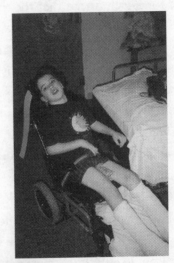

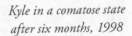
Kyle in a comatose state after six months, 1998

Kyle in a comatose state after eight months, 1998.

Chapter 19

After Kyle had casting done to his right arm to diminish the tight muscle tone, we noticed that the tension moved to his left arm. It was impossible to stop this muscle tone, but Kyle was right-handed, so if we had to pick an arm to work, we wanted the right one.

As Kyle became more alert, his muscle tone increased. Donna, his physical therapist, suggested we put Kyle in a body jacket to help his muscle tone and try to prevent his back from getting worse. She made the jacket of a white, solid plastic material with holes in it so Kyle's skin could breathe, and three straps held it on tight. It didn't look too comfortable, but I knew it was needed. Kyle had no strength in his upper body, and his legs were locked and could not bend at the knee. We noticed that his left side was not moving, but we hoped that with therapy his movement would come back.

We went to Children's Hospital and were admitted for surgery. Kyle was going to have a temporary Baclofen pump put in, in hopes that it would help his muscle tone. We would be there for a couple of days. If we noticed improvement, then surgery would take place to put in the permanent Baclofen pump.

While waiting in the pre-op area, I met many nurses and doctors, and everyone was wonderful to Kyle and me. Everything about the surgery was explained to me, and I asked if I could go in with him until he fell asleep. I walked to the room with Kyle, trying to be strong for him, telling him everything was going to be okay and that he was just going to go to sleep for a little while. I told him I would be right there when he woke up. I knew Kyle understood, but I wasn't sure how much. The room felt cold, and I was scared. This was all new to me. Kyle had already had several surgeries, but he hadn't been aware of them. I kissed him good-bye, and the nurse walked me out of the room. I cried, hoping this surgery would help him.

In the waiting room, alone and looking around, I saw women with their husbands. All I could think was, *why couldn't I have my husband?* This was so unfair. I needed Mike with me so badly. So I talked to him in my mind as if he was there with me. It may sound strange, but it helped me. I prayed a lot, and I know that gave me strength.

It was hard to be in Boston, as I didn't get to see my family much. One day a week I would get company, and then I would go home on Friday. My parents and family members came on the weekends, so Kyle wasn't alone. Other family members took care of my children at home. Everyone took a shift and helped out as much as they could. I was very fortunate to have two families always there for us.

Several hours went by, and Kyle was finally out of surgery, so I could go to see him. All wrapped up in a warm blanket, he looked so tiny. His weight was down to fifty pounds. Surgery had gone well, and now we would wait a few days to see the results. Kyle was on pain meds and seemed to be comfortable as we waited to be moved to a room.

Arriving on our floor, I walked through the halls and saw kids of all ages, some in cribs, and parents and nurses were very busy taking care of their patients. I couldn't believe how many sick little kids were there, but I knew I was in the best place imaginable. I met Kyle's nurse, and we went over all his medical history and medicine. Then we got Kyle settled and comfortable. The nurse told me that if I was staying overnight, the chair converted to a pullout bed. I was thankful, because I never left Kyle—especially in a hospital where no one knew him.

A physical therapist came in to evaluate Kyle on his muscle tone. She took measurements and said she would be back the next day to compare and see if his muscle tone had decreased.

Kyle's orthopedic doctor, Dr. Shapiro came to visit us. He was excited about the pump's potential to help Kyle's muscle tone. We couldn't fix his feet until we could get his muscle tone under control. He said to keep him updated.

Over the next few days, we noticed a little change in Kyle's tone. His body was handling the Baclofen, which was great news. Dr. Madsen and Dr. Berde decided that we could put in the permanent pump, and they scheduled the surgery to take place.

Off we went to surgery again. I went with Kyle to the operating room until he was asleep. I returned to the waiting room, full of excitement, knowing this was going to help him, though I wasn't sure how much. His spasms—and especially the sweating—had been getting worse, and I could only hope that this would somehow help him with his pain. The surgery took about four hours—a very long four hours for me. As I waited, I envied all the married couples and watched them holding hands and leaning on each other for support. I would have given anything for that. I wiped my tears.

Kyle was in the recovery room. He had done very well in surgery, and he was again wrapped up in warm blankets, sleeping peacefully. Waiting to see his gorgeous blue eyes, I hoped he wouldn't be in much pain. Dr. Berde explained to me that we would do some bolus feeds, with a sum of medicine all at once to help increase his dose more rapidly and hopefully that would help relieve his muscle tone and spasms. Then we would gradually increase the amount once a month until we knew he was comfortable. The problem with the Baclofen was that it could make Kyle sleepy, and he was still coming out of his coma and was sleepy as it was. We did a very gradual increase each month to make sure that it wasn't the Baclofen making him sleepy.

When we left the hospital and returned to Spaulding Rehab, I was looking forward to seeing how the next week would go. As Kyle recovered, I continued trying to feed him. He was getting stronger every day, but sometimes it took two hours just to eat some pudding.

After around two months of feeding Kyle, we were able to pull the feeding line out of his nose. Kyle had hated that line and always tried to pull it out, so we'd had to put big mittens on him and tie down his hand so he couldn't reach his nose. He'd had that tube for six months—luckily, with no infections. I was so thankful that we'd never put in the feeding tube. Kyle looked very happy to have this removed, and now he had one less problem. It was real progress, but the therapist and doctors warned me that I had to get in a certain amount of food each day or the line would have to go back in. I was determined that we could do it, and Kyle put his thumbs up!

I brought the girls to see Kyle that weekend. I wanted them to see their brother and observe that he could eat. It was important for the girls to see progress. Since I couldn't be with them during the week, I wanted them to know that my time away was helping their brother get better. Kim and Katie were so good with him. They sat on his bed or pushed him in his wheelchair down the hall. Sometimes they went outside by the water to feed the ducks.

The girls each took turns feeding Kyle. I showed them what to do. They were only four and six years of age, but if anyone had seen them with their brother, they would've thought the girls were much older than they were. I always tried to include the girls at every chance I had. I wanted them to stay close to Kyle and not be afraid of him. I was so blessed to still have my three children. I couldn't wait until we could be home again as a family. It had been seven long months.

Chapter 20

It was a beautiful day. Birds were chirping, flowers were budding, and I was excited to spend some quality time with my girls. We had decided to go out to eat at Papa Gino's and then to the Auburn Mall for some summer shopping. The girls were talking about their daddy and how much they missed him. They reminisced about how much they missed bath time, and Kimberly recalled doing little poops in the tub! She said, "Daddy would always yell for Mommy to help clean up the mess. He was so silly!" She giggled.

Katie said, "Daddy would come home, and we would greet him at the door. When he got on his knees to give us a kiss, we would take his card out of his shirt pocket and run and hide." She laughed. "Every day Daddy came and found us behind the rocking chair. Then we would go drink all his lemonade, and he would always tickle us and say, "You did it to me again! Remember that, Kim?" The girls laughed together, and it was so nice to hear them talking about their daddy.

I said, "Every morning before work, Daddy would put orange juice in a yellow cup for Katie, a red cup for Kim, and a blue cup for Kyle."

"He was so silly!" Katie said.

Kimberly asked, "Do you think Daddy can see us?"

"I sure hope so," I said. "Your daddy will never leave you. He will always be in your hearts. When you are sad or lonely, talk to him. It's okay. Mommy does it every day!"

Sitting down at Papa Gino's, our food was ready. I went to get our pizza. On the way back to the table, I noticed that Katie was talking to a man who was sitting by himself. I said, "Katie, come and eat."

The man walked over and said, "I am sorry about your loss. Your daughter just told me her daddy died in a car accident. She said she was in a body cast and had to learn how to walk again and that her brother is in a coma."

I was speechless; shocked that Katie had told a complete stranger what had happened to her. I said, "Thank you," feeling very uncomfortable.

Katie said, "Will you sit with me at my table?"

"Well, if your mother doesn't mind," the man replied.

Both girls said, "She doesn't mind."

I just smirked. The man sat down, and Katie climbed onto his lap. I didn't know what to do. It was obvious that she missed her father and the attention he'd given her.

I let them visit, and then Katie said, "Can we go to Friendly's and get ice cream?"

I said, "Sure, if that's what you would like to do."

Kim looked at the man and said, "Are you coming with us?"

Katie said, "Yes, he is!"

Off to Friendly's we went, and I felt very awkward. We had our ice cream, and then I said to the man, "Well, it was very nice meeting you, and thank you for being so polite to my little girls."

He said, "Anytime. They are so sweet." Then he said good-bye to the girls.

When we arrived at the mall, it was very busy. The girls picked out summer clothes and sandals. When they were done, I said, "Kyle needs clothes too! He has lost so much weight. Can you help me find some clothes for him?" They loved shopping for Kyle, and they knew he would love anything related to sports. It was a fun day, and it was so nice to be alone with my girls. It was like old times.

At home, I thought about Kyle's discharge meeting the next morning, where we would plan for Kyle to come home in two months. I was terrified of coming home with him. What if something went wrong? I wouldn't have the doctors and nurses right there. There were still lots of decisions to be made. How would I take care of him? My arm still didn't have much movement, and my fingers still wouldn't move, even with therapy five days a week. All I could hope for was that in the next two months I would heal a lot more. I had to stay focused on what needed to be done, one day at a time.

Reuben Rios, the man who had driven me to Boston so many times during these past five months, was outside honking for me. I loved my rides with him. He was like my personal shrink. I would tell him everything that was going on, and he would always give me good advice. We had become friends. He wouldn't just drop me off at Spaulding; he would come and say hi to Kyle a couple of times each week. It meant so much to me, and Kyle enjoyed seeing him. Telling Reuben about the big meeting that was going to take place, I was very nervous. He tried to keep me calm, saying, "It will all work out. Look how far you and Kyle have come. You will figure it out."

Later that day, Uncle Ronald, Aunt Gloria, Aunt Jean, and my parents came to attend the discharge meeting. We went in a big room with a huge table, where Dr. Rosenberg and therapist were seated. The doctor started off the meeting, stating that Kyle would be discharged in two months. They felt they couldn't do much more for him, and his discharge would come ten months after the accident. Kyle was still in a coma stage, but Dr. Rosenberg thought he didn't need more rehab. We were waiting to hear about the Massachusetts Hospital School in Canton, hoping they would accept Kyle in the fall.

The doctor looked at me and said, "I want to suggest a nursing home by Cape Cod for children Kyle's age—until you can care for him." We knew I still needed at least five more months of recovery for my arm, and I still wasn't sure what movement I would have.

I said, "A nursing home? No! He is coming home with me. We will work it out!"

She said, "We are fine with that, if Kyle goes home with the proper care and accessibility."

I said, "I will work it out. I will find a way."

Aunt Jean spoke up and said, "I live right next door. I will take care of Kyle, and other family members will help when needed."

The doctor said, "It has to be full-time care."

Jean said, "I will quit my job for a year and take care of Kyle." Dr. Rosenberg asked Jean if she could lift Kyle, and she said, "Yes, I can." The doctor explained that Jean would have to come and spend some days with Kyle to learn about his care before he arrived home, and she was fine with that. "Whatever I need to do, I will do," she replied.

"What about accessibility?" the doctor asked.

"We have only two steps to get in," I said.

"Is your bathroom accessible for a wheelchair?" the doctor asked.

I said, "No, it's very small." Dr. Rosenberg said it would need to be wheelchair accessible in order for Kyle to go home. When she asked about Kyle's bedroom, I said, "It was on the second floor, but I can put a hospital bed in the living room for now."

We talked about therapy. They would come to the house at first, and they would teach us everything we needed to do for Kyle at home. I felt good about that, because I already knew so much by observing. We talked about Kyle sleeping so much. They felt he needed to go back to the neurosurgeon to see if another shunt should be placed. He already had one, but they felt he might need one on the other side of his brain also. I didn't like to think about another surgery, but maybe it would help Kyle stay awake longer, and then maybe we would see more progress. The meeting ended, and I had to figure out how to make my bathroom accessible.

We lived in a four-family, side-by-side unit. My brother-in-law Norman and I owned the property. Mike's mom Rita, Aunt Jean, and I lived there, each in our own units. I went home that night thinking about what Mike had always told me. He'd said that someday he wanted to move into his mother's apartment and build an extension on the house. Then we wouldn't be cramped with the kids. He figured she lived alone, so she wouldn't mind just moving next door. I would just listen to him, never saying much. Yeah, it would have been nice, but I'd never thought it would happen. I talked to Norman about an accessible bathroom, and he said it couldn't be done. So I said, "Well, then, I guess I need to do an addition to your mom's house—if she agrees to move into my house." It was the only way to keep Kyle from being sent to a nursing home.

Meme Rita was in her rocking chair, holding her tea and looking out the window. I asked her about doing the addition so I could take Kyle home. She was wonderful and said, "Whatever we need to do is fine with me." She wanted Kyle home, not in a nursing home. She always said, "The poor kid. I feel so bad for him! I pray every day for his pain to go away."

I felt awful making her leave her home, but I also knew I didn't have a choice. I started to look for a contractor that same night. Within a week, I found one who said they could start immediately. I was thrilled. Larry Brunelle came to the house, and we drew up some plans. I had to get it approved by the town, and Larry said he would hire the electricians and plumbers. He would do it all. What a relief it was for me! I could concentrate on everything else I needed to do.

I went back to Spaulding and told the staff I was building an addition on the house. It would have an accessible bathroom, a raised tub, bedrooms on the main floor and second floor, and lifts in the ceiling. There would be a stair lift so Kyle could get to his bedroom at night, and my room was close by. There would also be a handicap ramp outside. The only problem was that it would never be ready in June—maybe by late August.

Everyone agreed that this arrangement would be fine, because it was in the works. Kyle could come home! I was thrilled, relieved, and especially thankful for Aunt Jean. If she hadn't helped me out, Kyle would have had to go to the nursing home, or I would have had to hire someone full-time.

Chapter 21

Our time at Spaulding was coming to an end, and I sat with Kyle outside, feeding the ducks. Kyle was making some sounds and using thumbs up for yes and down for no. We knew he understood everything we said, but we were still trying to figure out where he was as far as grade level. My mom was a teacher, and she was doing some testing on Kyle. She used a lot of flash cards, colored pictures, and shapes. She was shocked that Kyle new so much, with his type of brain injury. We had been told that he would be a vegetable, so we felt very lucky to have what we did.

Kyle tried hard to talk, but nothing made sense. Then he would try to spell, and that was how we communicated. With so much impulsivity, it took him a while just to get one word out. It was like having a baby again. I knew what he wanted by the little sounds he made and by his facial expressions. We learned a little sign language to help with feelings like *hungry, thirsty, bored,* and *I love you.* Overall, we did well, and it all came together.

Kyle spelled out *dad.* I had mentioned to him before that Daddy had died in the accident, and we listened to his music every day, but I could tell that he wanted more. I asked him, "Do you want me to tell you what happened at the accident? Do you want to hear about what happened to you?" His thumb went up.

I explained that we had been coming home from the Auburn Mall, when someone who was driving on the other side of the road hit us. The driver had been on cocaine and had had some alcohol in his system. Daddy had been hurt really bad. The steering wheel had crushed him, and he'd died instantly. I told Kyle that he had been sitting behind Daddy. Katie had fractured her hip, but Kimberly had been okay. I said that I had hurt my arm and back but that I was healing just like he was. When Daddy saw the truck coming at us, he had turned the wheel and saved all of our lives. He loved us so much! I told Kyle that he had hurt his head and received a brain injury. The doctors had said he would die or be a vegetable. I said, "You're no vegetable, that's for sure," and I gave him a hug.

Aunt Jean went to the hospital during the final two weeks to learn how to care for Kyle, which went well. Construction started on the house. Lazo's Construction donated their time and material to put in our foundation, which only took a few days, and then the building started. It all went up fast, and Rita lived in her house until the very end of the project. I loved going home and seeing the progress.

We had two appointments at Children's Hospital. The first was with neurosurgery. We talked about putting in another shunt, and Dr. Madsen agreed that it should be done. It would keep Kyle more alert, and then we could hope to see more progress. We agreed that it would be done in June.

Our second appointment was with Kyle's neurologist. Dr. Darras couldn't believe that Kyle was more alert and was waking up more, eating pureed foods, and trying hard to communicate. The doctor explained to me that a stroke patient normally recovered the most during the first year. After that, there would still be gains, but not as much.

Kyle was different, though. He was a miracle. He wasn't supposed to have been able to do anything. He was not even supposed to have short—or long-term memory—and he had both. Looking at Kyle's MRI, his progress didn't make sense. I remember Dr. Darras saying to me, "Anything he does is a blessing. Keep doing what you are doing."

I chuckled and explained that we were constantly doing school activities with Kyle—nursery rhymes, ABCs, and anything that we thought he could do. I said, "It takes me hours each day to feed him, but he's getting stronger. My goal is for Kyle to be able to feed himself and to sip from a straw in the next year."

Dr. Darras smiled at me and said, "Keep up the good work. See you in a few months."

Getting Kyle ready for bed at Spaulding Rehab, I started to tell him about the day I'd met his daddy at United Lens. Kyle just looked at me with his big blue eyes. "I dropped you of at Auntie Laurie's every morning and went to work," I said. "I met Daddy in the crib (an office) and was introduced to him by Cheryl. He was very sweet. He shook my hand and said he would be glad to help me if I ever needed anything or had a question. Cheryl chuckled at that. I worked on the first floor in one of the offices, and Mike was a production control supervisor.

"Every day I went down by the soda machines to get drinks for the girls in my office, and Mike always came by and said hi. That was where we became friends and got to know each other. I told him I had a little boy that was one year old and that I had just left my husband a few months ago and was waiting to go to court. Over time, I shared more with him, and he shared that he was single. He said he had gotten out of a bad relationship a few months earlier.

"Six months went by, and he knew I was dating. I had just stopped seeing someone, so he called me and asked if I would like to go running. He was training for the Fourth-of-July race, and since I'd told him I used to run in high school, he thought I might still run. I said okay. I thought of him as a friend, and I knew he was a really nice guy. He was nine years older than me, but he was a gentleman. I didn't like his beard. It was so hairy, it hid his face, and I was petrified of it!

"Saturday afternoon on the day of our run, I heard a knock at my door, and it was Mike. I was scared, as I hadn't run in years. You ran to the door and opened it, and right away Mike got on his hands and knees and asked you if you wanted a horsey ride. You said yes with a big smile, and before I knew it, you were on Daddy's back, laughing, and Daddy was making noises like a horse.

"It was so nice to see you so happy, but it was time for us to go, so we brought you to the sitter, my neighbor downstairs. Off Daddy and I went, running. We didn't get too far, as we both were tired and the weather wasn't the best. We went to get some food, and then Daddy brought me home. Daddy said, 'Thank you for coming out. I had a great time. Maybe next week we can do something.' I said, 'Yes, that sounds great.' Then I said good-night and went inside my house."

Kyle still looked wide-awake, wanting to hear more, so I went on. "Daddy and I went out a few more times. The only problem was that he always wore the same pants and sweater. They were so ugly! His pants were gray suede. His sweater was dark green, and his sleeves ended a little above his wrist, because it was way too small. When he had it on again for our third date, I didn't know what to do. It looked awful!" Kyle took in every word I was saying and gave me little smiles.

"We left for our date, and Daddy needed to stop at his house first. He asked me, 'Do you want to see my place? I just redid it and moved in.' I said, 'Sure,' thinking that once I had him inside his place, I was going to have him change clothes. I said, 'Don't you have another sweater?' He said, 'What's wrong with this one?' I said, "It's too small, and it's the third time you've worn it!' He laughed and said, 'I'll put something else on.'

"Daddy ended up putting on some khakis with a nice long-sleeved shirt. He looked so much better. He didn't know how to roll up his sleeves, but he looked good. His apartment was gorgeous, all hardwood floors and black leather furniture—a really nice bachelor pad." Kyle really was listening and wanted more!

"My life really changed, and dating Daddy was the best decision I'd ever made. He was so good to you, and he treated me so special. Dating was hard for me. I didn't like to leave you, because I was gone all week at work. Daddy understood that, and he respected me for it. After that, all our plans included you, and we did everything as a little family. It took me months to get really close to Daddy, though. I was shy and scared, but he was always a gentleman and said that I should let him know when I was ready. After many months together, I finally said I was ready, and we had a beautiful night together. It felt so right.

"I was falling for Daddy, and I knew you just loved him. He always planned special things to do on the weekends. Whether he took us to the circus, the zoo, or bowling, it was always special, and every summer he took us on a nice vacation. Financially, I was barely making it, and Daddy knew I couldn't afford anything extra, but he never cared about that. He paid for everything. Kyle, do you remember that our big night was on Thursday? You and I would go have pizza, because that was all I could afford." Kyle looked at me with his thumbs up.

"My divorce went through, and I was so glad to end that chapter of my life. I knew I deserved better, and I knew I'd found a man who treated me special and was mature and responsible. I had been with Mike for a year and a half, and everything was perfect in my eyes. We got along so well and were very happy together. I loved his family, and they all accepted you from day one. My family thought Mike was wonderful.

"Kyle, do you remember when you and Daddy were sitting in a chair having a pop, and you looked at him and said, 'Can I call you Daddy?' Daddy looked at you and said, 'I don't mind, but you have to ask your Mommy.' I was in the kitchen, listening, in shock. You yelled to me and said, 'Can I call Mike Daddy?' I looked at Mike with big eyes, and Mike said, 'I don't mind. I love him, and I'm not going anywhere.' In my heart, I knew that we were going to be together, so I said, 'Well, Kyle, if that's what you want to do, that is fine with me.' You looked up at Daddy with your blue eyes and said, 'Hi, Daddy,' and Daddy just tickled you. It was so sweet it brought me to tears.

"Daddy was nine years older than I was, and I was told often that he would never marry. I didn't believe that, because I knew I had something so special with him, but I had to make sure. One day at work, I said to him, 'You know, we have been together for two years now, and I want to know if we are ever going to get married. If we aren't, I am moving on.' He was in shock. 'Moving on!' he said. 'You mean you would break up with me?' I said, 'Yes, I want to get married and have more children. If that's not in your plans, I don't want to waste my time.' He said, 'When I come over tonight, we will talk about it.' I said, 'No, you can stay home tonight and think about it and let me know tomorrow.' I walked away, feeling good that I'd said something, because I really wanted to know my future.

"The next day, I went down to the soda machine, and Daddy came over. I said, 'So, did you think about it?' He said, 'Of course I did,' and I said, 'Well?' He said, 'Lisa, it was only two more weeks. You ruined my surprise! I booked a hotel in Boston, and I was going to take you to the diamond building so you could pick out your diamond. Here's my bankbook. You can see that I have been saving for it every week.'

"I was speechless. I felt so bad and was in shock, but I was so relieved because I loved him so much. I had to go back upstairs, and he said, 'Can I come over tonight?' I smiled and said, 'You'd better!'

"We went to Boston for the night, just as he'd planned, and we found a gorgeous diamond. I was the happiest girl ever. I had found my Prince Charming. We started to plan our wedding, and both sides of the family were excited. Daddy's family was shocked that he was going to settle down and get married. They'd always thought he wouldn't, but Daddy just didn't want to get married only to get divorced. He wanted it all and wouldn't settle for less.

"I'd gotten an annulment from your biological father so I could get married again in a church. It was tough, with plenty of bad memories, but I was happy I'd done it. Daddy and I went through the Pre-Cana course at the Catholic Church, and we enjoyed it. We were so much alike, and our birthdays were only a day apart from each other.

"The year went by fast, with lots of planning. Picking out my dress was so much fun. I felt like a princess dressed in white with a long train and lots of ruffles. My sisters and my friend Evelyn were in the wedding. Mike had Norman, his brother, as best man and some friends as ushers. You were four years old and were the ring bearer, and my niece Holly was the flower girl. You were both so adorable. Holly wouldn't go down the aisle, so you ended up giving me away with my dad. Walking down the aisle, I was so happy and feeling so lucky to be marrying someone I was so in love with—and more importantly, someone who was so good to my son.

"When my father and I reached Mike, you went over to Mike, grabbed his leg, and stayed with us through the whole service. When we exchanged vows, my voice became different, as I was fighting tears. You looked up at me, making sure I was okay. Mike and I were so happy. We'd done it! We had become Mr. and Mrs. Michael Brodeur. It was one of the best days of my life!"

I kissed Kyle goodnight and said, "The day I had you was also one of the best days of my life. I love you more than anything. Did you know that you are my favorite son?"

Kyle responded with his thumbs up and a little sound. I knew what he wanted to say to me was, "No shit. I'm your only son." Kyle just tried to smile and held his thumbs up!

Chapter 22

I tried to prepare myself to leave the rehab center that had become a home for Kyle and me, but it was really sad and difficult. After being at Spaulding for almost eight months, I thought we would have been excited to leave. Instead, I was nervous and worried that I couldn't handle it if anything went wrong with Kyle medically without a doctor nearby. The doctors went over everything with me, especially his therapies, exercises, and the strengthening he needed. I felt good about all the information. I had seen it done so often that it was embedded in my head.

I was mostly worried about Kyle's spasms, as they were definitely getting worse, and the sweating was unbearable. Kyle would soak through his sheets in five minutes. I would put a pad and then a sheet on his bed, trying to keep him cooler. He couldn't bear to wear clothes or have anything touching his legs—especially his feet. He cried out in pain, and the spasms were intolerable. I tried to massage his legs, but it was so difficult, and it went on for hours. With my back in severe pain and my arm in a removable hand cast, it was difficult to massage Kyle properly. In tears, I did the best I could, praying that this was just a stage that would pass. How could Kyle live in all this pain? I just kept praying and never gave up hope. Tomorrow had to be a better day.

The day I was dreading had arrived, and we were leaving Spaulding. I was in tears as we said our good-byes, and everyone wished us the best of luck and reassured me that I would be okay. We were off to Children's

Hospital in Boston by ambulance to have another surgery. I told Kyle that after this surgery we were going home sweet home. I couldn't believe it. It had been ten months! I explained to him that he was getting an extension to the shunt he already had, hoping it would help him to stay more awake and be more alert. Then we hoped he would start to wake up more from his coma, and we would see more progress. I asked Kyle if that sounded good, and he gave me thumbs up.

Morning arrived, and Kyle was off to surgery again. This routine had become familiar, but it never got easier. I walked into the surgical suite dressed in my blue scrubs and held Kyle's hand until he was asleep. I cried as I left him. I just couldn't get use to this. I had been through it several times now, but it still felt like the first time. He was my little boy—so strong and handsome—and together we were determined to win this battle. So far, we were winning, and Kyle was still fighting alongside me. Most importantly, he was not a vegetable!

Several hours had passed, and Dr. Madson approached me. The surgery had gone well, and Kyle was doing great. The doctor really felt like this was going to help, and his positive thinking gave me so much hope. After seeing Kyle, all bundled up with bandages on his head and sleeping peacefully, I called home. I let everyone know that Kyle was doing well and that we hoped to be home in a few days. My girls were so happy. I heard them in the background, saying, "A few more days and Mommy and Kyle will be home for good!" That made me so excited to get home. My girls gave me some normalcy in life. Saying the word *home* was starting to feel so good, and I looked forward to not rushing off to a hospital every day. I would actually be able to help my girls with their needs and spend some much-needed time with them.

I asked to see Dr. Berde to see if we could increase his Baclofen pump. Kyle's spasms were frequent and intolerable, and the sweating was getting worse. The doctor agreed to an increase, explaining that every couple of weeks I could come back for adjustments as needed. Also, he would send me home with Valium to try to comfort Kyle. I was relieved that I would have some medicine. I just hoped it would work or at least make him sleep so he wouldn't be hollering in pain.

Kyle was doing very well—no fevers or low-grade temperature—so we got the okay to go home. I couldn't believe we were going home after ten and a half months. We gathered our belongings together and filled all Kyle's prescriptions at Children's Hospital. The nurse came and said that the paramedics were there to bring us home. Looking at Kyle, I said, "Let's go home and see your sisters!"

It was a long ride. One hour and fifteen minutes later, we arrived home. Meme Rita, Aunt Jean, Uncle Ronald, and Aunt Gloria were waiting to greet us. The paramedics brought Kyle into the house and put him in his hospital bed in the living room. Kyle looked so happy; I could tell that he recognized his home.

Everything about the house was different from the way it had been. Before the accident, we had bought new furniture that Kyle had picked out. It came in two weeks after the accident happened, so Mike never even got to see it. We had to store it at Jordan's Furniture until we no longer needed the three hospital beds in the living room. The furniture had finally been delivered two months later.

Kyle just looked around as everyone greeted him, and I could tell he was happy. The girls jumped in bed with him, being silly but careful not to hurt him. Kyle had a lot of impulsivity going on, and he was flicking his mouth—a new development in the past month. There wasn't anything I could do about it. I only hoped it would be a short stage.

Kyle's aunts and uncles came to visit. It was really nice—and especially nice for him to see his cousins. It was hard on the kids, because he couldn't play with them, and he was not the Kyle they knew. It was an adjustment for everyone.

Our first night at home went well until around midnight, when the spasms started. Once the spasms started, they were hard to stop. Kyle just cried in pain. I gave him the Valium, but it only helped a little. I was like a drug store, having so many medicines. Kyle needed twenty-two pills a day, given every couple of hours throughout the day and night. I slept on the couch so I could be with him. Sometimes I was lucky if I got an hour between his spasms to shut my eyes. I knew that we would be increasing his Baclofen pump in a week, and I couldn't wait for that appointment.

Every morning, Aunt Jean washed and dressed Kyle and put his body jacket on him. Then she lifted him to his chair. Several times a day, he had to go back into bed to rest and to have a diaper change. It was a lot of lifting, but she never complained, not even once. I was so lucky to have her. Now that I was home, I got to help more with the girls. Between Jean and me, we kept very busy, as Kyle's care was a full-time job—especially preparing his meals, which had to be pureed and soft. Feeding took about two hours for one meal. I stopped going to therapy for my arm, as I had no time. I did the exercises at home.

Kyle was starting to be more alert; the shunt surgery had helped. We noticed that he could stay awake longer, trying to talk, getting out sounds. He even managed a half smile. We had a speech therapist come to our house. Our goals were to strengthen his face muscles so he could do a full smile and to teach him to stick out his tongue and make noises. Hopefully, in the months to come, he would even be able to sip out of a straw. We were starting from the beginning, but we had a lot of hope. I was never going to give up!

I bought a new Dodge van with a handicap lift with the funds that people had contributed to our family after the accident. What a blessing the van was! It was so nice to be able to take Kyle to his appointments and to go out with my girls as a family.

We took our first trip out on a gorgeous afternoon. Kyle didn't want to go out, as his life was so different now and the pain was so bad. He just wanted to stay home in bed. I told him, "I know life is different, but it doesn't mean we stop living. We need to go out and enjoy life. You will love a little ride in your new van. We are going." Kyle pointed his thumb down, unhappy with me, and the girls tried to console him, telling him it would be okay.

I had a side entry for Kyle to enter the van. The only problem was that I still didn't have the use of my left arm. It was difficult to move his chair to position it in the middle of the van. The girls, only four and six years old, helped me to move Kyle's chair into place. I taught them how to buckle his chair in. I was amazed at how much help they were at such a young age.

Off we went. At the first set of lights, I took a turn, and Kyle's chair tilted some. I had to stop, and the girls and I adjusted the straps. We were learning. We just rode around town and then stopped for ice cream. It felt good to be out of the house. Kyle seemed to enjoy himself and wasn't mad at me any longer. Later that day, when we arrived home, I told him that he needed to get out once a day, whether it was outside in the yard, on a simple walk, or going somewhere together. It was healthy and good for all of us. He just looked at me without responding, but I knew he had enjoyed the ride.

Kyle started to adjust to going out and being more alert. He started to ask questions about where he had been taken after the accident and how long he had been in the hospital. I told him he had been at U-Mass Hospital in Worcester, Massachusetts, for two full months and that he had left on December 26, 1997, the day after Christmas. He didn't remember those days. He asked me if I could take him there and show him where his room was and meet the doctor and nurses that had taken care of him. Shocked, I said, "Of course I will take you. I bet they will be happy to see you." I called U-Mass and set up a time to go there. They were thrilled to hear that Kyle wanted to visit.

The next day, we went. I experienced so many emotions as we walked into the hospital. It had only been fifteen months since the accident. In the elevator, I pressed the button for the Pediatric ICU floor. I pushed Kyle's chair over to the nurse's station and asked for his nurse Martha and Dr. Wood. They both came around the corner and hugged me tight, happy to see Kyle. The doctor and nurses looking at Kyle in awe amazed that he was alive and alert. Kyle looked up at them with his big, blue eyes and spelled out, "Thank you for saving my life."

Wiping his tears, Dr. Wood told Kyle and me that they had always wondered if they had done the correct thing, saving his life, but now he knew they had. He said thank you to Kyle. Knowing where Kyle was today made the doctor feel good inside.

I'd had no idea that Kyle was going to say thank you. I was just as shocked as they were! What a great visit! I was so thankful that my son felt like this. In fifteen months, he'd already had ten surgeries. I was amazed that he felt this way, even with all his pain and spasms. What a courageous son I had! Holding my head up high, I left there feeling proud.

Chapter 23

Our addition was coming along nicely. It was all framed, and the electrical and plumbing were showing progress. It was nice being home, and I could see the changes daily. Many questions from the contractors always awaited me, but I loved it. It was such a change from medical decisions and hospitals.

While the job was being done, I often talked to Lenny, one of the electricians. We became friends, and he always asked me about Kyle. It was nice having someone to talk to. I shared a lot with him over the months, especially about missing my husband and about what I was going through with Kyle. Lots of conversations ended in tears. I could tell that he cared and couldn't imagine going through this with his daughter Cassie. He shared things about his life with me. I listened, encouraging him to move on and assuring him that he would find some happiness in time.

School was about to come to an end for the year, and Kyle had missed most of his fifth year at his school. Mr. Jim Kane, Kyle's teacher, knew that Kyle had arrived home the week before, and he called to see if his students could take a class trip to our house and put on a skit. I said sure. Kyle and I were excited to see all his classmates.

Two weeks after the phone call, Kyle's classmates and teachers came over. Aunt Jean brought Kyle outside in his wheelchair, dressed in shorts and a body jacket over his shirt. His legs were straight out, his feet twisted and his hair short, and there were scars on his head from

A Mother's *Journey*

THROUGH FAITH, HOPE, AND COURAGE

Lisa Brodeur

A Mother's Journey

Through Faith, Hope, and Courage

By Lisa Brodeur

This is the story of an incredible and inspirational journey of a mother dedicated to her three children. She was determined to survive a tragic event through faith, hope, and courage.

The mother was severely injured, and her devoted husband and father of her children was killed instantly. She watched her son fight for every breath; he took to survive. Her daughters, only three and five years old, were traumatized. The young girls screamed in pain and wondered where their father and brother were.

The mother buried her husband, stood by strongly as her son had surgery after surgery, and went to court to see that the man who changed their lives forever was served with justice. She tried to stay strong and focused for her children. She wasn't able to grieve the loss of her husband. She made endless medical decisions and stayed with her son in the hospital for many months. She waited to see progress from her comatose son and saw her little girls only on weekends. The girls trying to adjust emotionally and physically to their new life.

This book will make someone think about his or her choices. Making the wrong choice, like doing drugs or driving intoxicated, can have a lasting impact on your life and the lives of others. Someone else's choices caused this mother's family to go on a journey that no one should ever have to endure.

Check out Lisa's Book, Presentation, Videos and Reviews

Web: WWW.LisaBrodeur.com
Facebook: A Mother's Journey
Twitter.com Lisa Brodeur
Phone: 774-253-0492

the surgeries. He was twenty pounds lighter and he exhibited lots of impulsivity and flicking of his mouth. The kids were in shock when they saw Kyle. They hadn't known what to expect. They only knew that he was their friend, that he had survived, and that he would never be the same.

The children had made a "welcome home" sign, and they had all written nice messages to Kyle. Kyle looked at his classmates, wanting to speak, but he couldn't get anything out. He was frustrated but happy to see his friends. I explained to the kids that Kyle could hear and understand them but had trouble communicating back.

The kids were great. They just wanted to put on a skit for Kyle and make him happy. The skit was excellent. In the skit, Mr. Kane had given his students an assignment to write a paper about a person of significance, someone who had affected the world today through their achievements or accomplishments. One student couldn't decide whom to write about. She went to sleep that night and dreamed of meeting and talking with many famous persons, each portrayed by other class members, such as Neil Armstrong, Martin Luther King Jr., Bob Dylan, Walt Disney, and many others. The student carefully considered each one, but there was one individual she considered above them all. She chose someone—not from the sixties but from the nineties—who had, in her eyes, shown great courage and a will to never give up. She chose her classmate, Kyle Brodeur!

That short skit carried such a important lesson for us all. It said that the world was a better place because of one young boy whose life had touched the lives of many—family, friends, neighbors, teachers, and classmates. Knowing Kyle reminded us all to take time to care, to love, to pray, to go on in spite of difficulties, and to be thankful, knowing that each of us can make a difference in this world.

The kids had put a lot of effort and time into making this visit perfect for Kyle. I couldn't thank Mr. Kane enough for doing this for us. What a great teacher! And Kyle loved him. It was sad when our visit was over. I told the kids to stop by anytime they liked. Kyle would love to have company. The kids saying their goodbye while some are in tears.

They couldn't believe what they had seen, and they knew their friend would never be the same.

One afternoon, my girlfriend Natalie came down and invited me to go out dancing with her and her husband. She thought it would be good for me, since I hadn't done anything in eleven months. I wanted to go, but I was scared. I said, "I don't have the clothes. I haven't gone to a club in many years." Natalie said, "Then we are going shopping. You need to go somewhere besides hospitals and do something for yourself."

I knew I needed a mental change. I missed my husband and best friend, always thinking about how my life had changed. Having to make medical decisions so often, life was different for me. I was always dealing with court, spasms, surgeries, and weekly appointments in Boston. I was trying to keep my girls busy and happy, and my injuries were still healing. I knew Natalie was right.

We went shopping, and I got some jeans and sandals. I must say, I had a great time shopping, and I even had a great time being out. At first it felt funny. I felt like I didn't belong. But then I adjusted, and I even danced. It was good for me. It opened up my eyes to realize that I had to make myself happy in order to be the kind of mother that I needed to be.

It was hard on my family when I started to go out. They thought I was on the rebound and just wanted to meet someone. I totally understood them, but what they didn't realize was that I wasn't looking for a man or a relationship. I just wanted a friend, someone from the outside to talk to once in a while. My sister set me up with someone, and I went on a date at the casino. It was the longest day. He was nice, but he wasn't my type and didn't have the same interests.

I met someone from the club who was not really the type to settle down with, but he could make me laugh. I had seen him a couple of times, but when I realized that he wanted more than a friend, I said good-bye. I really wasn't looking for a relationship, and I realized that men just didn't want a friend. It was difficult to imagine myself with someone other than Michael. I used to remind myself of one thing that

Mike had said: "Life is for the living." It's a very true statement, but it's very hard to act on it when you are missing the one you love so badly.

I went over to look at the new addition. It was looking good and was almost finished. I talked to Lenny and shared my dating experiences with him. He seemed to completely understand where I was emotionally. Lenny was the kind of friend I was really looking for. He was a gentleman, and he wasn't making passes at me. We acted like friends.

One day when I was there, Lenny's friend said, "You two should go out sometime." I didn't know what to say. Deep down, I thought I would go. Lenny was really sweet. We had known each other for two months, and we always enjoyed talking to each other. I just looked down, embarrassed. Lenny smiled and said, "When the job is done, I would love to take you out." I was embarrassed and walked away, very nervous. I realized then that I really would like to go out with him, and I hoped he would ask me out when the job was done. I knew that if we did go out, it would be pleasant. He already knew my situation and me already. I knew we would have a good time.

Lenny waited until the last week of the job's completion before asking me out. Nervously, I agreed to go. The family seemed to be okay with it, because everyone knew him. Off we went in Lenny's car. We were both nervous. Lenny was dressed in jeans, shirt, and work boots. He worried about how he looked and whether his car was clean enough. I told him not to worry, that everything was fine. We had a great time. We went out to eat and then watched a movie, *Titanic*. We had a great, relaxing night, with no pressure. It felt so nice to do something relaxing and to have great company. He brought me home and gave me a kiss goodnight. I was excited to see him the next day on the job.

That night, Kyle had a bad night with lots of spasms. I stayed up with him for hours, trying to massage his legs and putting cold towels on his forehead. I realized that I couldn't be gone for so long. Kyle needed me here at home.

Lenny called the next day, wanting to see me. I explained to him that I wanted to go, but I couldn't, because Kyle wasn't doing well.

Lenny asked if he could come and sit with Kyle and me. The girls were already sleeping. I said okay, that I would be up most of the night anyway, and it would be nice to have company. Lenny arrived and stayed by Kyle's bed, rubbing and massaging his leg, trying to break the spasms. Eventually Kyle fell asleep. I was in a lot of pain myself by then, and Lenny massaged my neck and back. It felt so good, and I thought how nice it was to have someone take care of me. I was so thankful I had a special friend, but I also realized that I was starting to have feelings for him.

Every night thereafter, Lenny came over to keep me company. It was easier to stay home than to go out. Life was just too busy. I felt very lucky to have met someone I enjoyed talking to, someone with whom I could share my feelings about Mike. I knew that Lenny and I enjoyed being together and were becoming a couple.

Lenny wanted me to meet his little girl. Actually, his little girl was nine years old and was almost as tall as me. I laughed when I met her. The way he had described her, I'd thought she was little. Cassie was beautiful and pleasant and had a very nice smile. I heard a lot about her. Kimberly and Katie met her, and they played well together. Cassie was very good to Kyle. She would lie in bed with him and do whatever she could to make him happy.

Our addition was complete, so we could move in. I was very excited that it was done, but I was also sad to leave my home with Mike. My mother-in-law, Rita, would be living there now. That was good for me, as I could still come back and visit. I was excited to have a bedroom and a bed to sleep on. I had been sleeping on a couch in the living room for two months, with Kyle on a hospital bed.

In our new place, we put a bedroom upstairs for Kyle. I duplicated his old bedroom exactly, from wallpaper to rug, with the same decorations. I wanted him to remember his room and to feel like he was home. Kimberly and Katie picked out new bedspreads and rug colors with matching paint. They loved their rooms. Kyle had a lift to go up and down the stairs, and we had a room for him downstairs during the day. It was great and had lots of windows. We put in a handicap bathroom downstairs with a raised tub. Aunt Jean didn't have to lift Kyle now, as we had purchased a Barrier Free Lift with tracking in the ceiling. With the press of a button, the kids and I could transfer Kyle very easily. Jean still preferred to carry him sometimes for the transfers. The kitchen was all remodeled—floors, cabinets, and wallpaper. There were three bathrooms and a very nice living room. It all came out gorgeous.

We purchased a hot tub for Kyle and me. It was good therapy for both of us. The hot tub relaxed his muscles and helped with spasms. We put an addition on the deck near the pool so that Kyle could watch his sisters swim. We tried to make everything as easy as we could with the wheelchair.

The girls wanted to go swimming and jumped in the water while Kyle and I were watching them. Katie said, "Mommy, when you were at Spaulding with Kyle, I was swimming, and I wouldn't get out of the pool when Meme and Aunt Jean told me to. I started to cry for you because I missed you, and Meme had to jump in and get me." She giggled.

I said, "I know. I couldn't believe your seventy-eight-year-old grandmother jumped in with all her clothes on to get you. You girls are so silly." Kyle loved that story and tried to smile.

Chapter 24

Kyle was accepted to the Massachusetts Hospital School in Canton, Massachusetts. It was such a wonderful school with so many opportunities for him. I knew this school was the one and only school for Kyle. The hard thing was that it was like sending my child off to college at a very young age. Kyle would leave me on a Sunday night and come home on Friday afternoon. When he started in the fall, I followed the bus to school and stayed with Kyle on Sunday night for a few hours. I went back on Wednesday night and again on Friday. I did that for years. I had visited this school back in the winter with my brother-in-law John, my sister Laurie, and my parents, so I knew it was a very special school. I realized that if Kyle was going to learn and grow, he needed people who specialized in this field. It was going to be a very hard road, but like my mom always said, "It's called tough love."

Entering the school through the admissions office on the first day was very scary. This scene was all new for me. Everyone was very pleasant, and after being admitted and signing many forms, we were brought to where Kyle would sleep and eat and spend his evenings. It was a cottage called Bailey's, and Kyle shared a room with a group of boys. I loved the idea that he wouldn't be alone and that someone would always be around to help if needed. Kyle couldn't speak, but some of his roommates could. I was hoping they would make friends with Kyle and all look out for one another.

I stayed overnight the first couple of days, making sure that they knew what to do if Kyle had spasms and seeing if they knew how to position him. I stayed in the foyer on a chair, jumping up often to check on Kyle. I was nervous, and I was trying to prepare myself to eventually leave and trust these wonderful people with my son.

Kyle was starting to communicate more by spelling, and he was staying more alert. He was able to enjoy going out more, and he started to make friends and get to know the staff. He had a very busy schedule, with lots of therapies, class, art, music, and computers. After school, before or after supper, he had recreation. That would involve a sport, bowling, swimming, a radio station, art, cooking, or animal care. Every couple of months, the activities changed, so he always had different things to do. This school offered everything and anything I could think of. There was no time for any student to get bored.

I have to say that it took many months for all of my family to adjust to Kyle not being home during the week. Kyle had the biggest adjustment, as he had to learn to trust so many people and be without me for the first time. Every Wednesday, the girls and I went to visit Kyle after school. The girls never complained about the ride being an hour and a half long. They just wanted to see their brother. Our visits were so nice, and my girls and I made many friends with the staff and kids. My children learned at a very young age about "special needs" and that everyone was different but unique, special in his or her own way. Kimberly and Katie were always so kind and sweet with all the kids. No matter what the disability was, they interacted with everyone. The girls had many questions at times, and I always answered them as truthfully as I could. The kids at MHS loved Wednesdays, they knew Kimberly and Katie would be visiting. The girls always had a lot of fun, as the people at the school had become another family for us.

Life was very busy, and Lenny moved in with us. Kyle had started his new school. Kimberly started third grade at her new school, and Katie started first grade at her school. Kimberly was very nervous about starting school, as she was still having trouble talking. The therapist said it could take years for her to overcome this. We had to be patient and try to keep her calm. It was hard to not be overwhelmed in our life.

Each day with Kyle had brought different problems, but now we were dealing with the adjustment of not having Kyle home every day. The girls missed him. We called Kyle at night to say goodnight, but Kyle couldn't talk. It didn't matter to the girls; as long as they knew Kyle was on the other end, they were happy. I heard them giggling and saying silly stuff to him and even singing him songs by the Back Street Boys and Spice Girls—anything to make him happy.

Katie was fine with starting school. She was so excited to see her friends and meet her teacher. She always had so much to tell everyone about her brother. Kim was more reserved and quiet. She liked her teacher and was excited about making friends. The girls loved it when Lenny's daughter, Cassie, came over and spent the weekend. They played very nicely together and had lots of fun. They always danced and sang for Kyle and put on shows for him. They definitely knew how to make him laugh.

The girls decided that they wanted to continue taking dance and Pop Warner cheering this year. We were very busy, but it was a good and healthy busy—especially on weekends, going to practice and football games. Kyle loved it. He loved football and made friends. It was nice to be able to be there for my girls and do what a mom should do.

The holidays arrived, and it was nice having Kyle home. He had missed last Christmas while he was in the hospital. We did our tradition, with Santa bringing in the presents and doing something funny to make the kids laugh. Santa ate cookies and drank his milk while making loud noises. Cassie, Kimberly, and Katie laughed as they tried to be quiet, and Kyle watched Santa in amazement with his hand over his mouth. Everyone seemed to enjoy the event, as the girls hid on the stairs and Kyle sat in his wheelchair, covered with a blanket. Then the girls rushed to bed and closed their eyes before Santa flew over the house with his reindeer.

On Christmas morning, after the presents were open, I took my three kids aside and told them I had a very special present for them in remembrance of their Daddy. They looked at me with big eyes, wondering what it could be. I gave them each a present and explained to them that Daddy couldn't be there with us but that he was with us in our hearts and would never leave us. Daddy loved us, and he was watching over us from heaven. They opened their presents with big smiles on their faces. Inside were T-shirts with pictures of them with their father, and they loved them. All three kids said it was their favorite Christmas present, and they wore their shirts to bed that night.

Missing Mike never seemed to go away for me. I was always thinking of him and talking to him daily. I was trying to find happiness in my life, but I could never let go or forget my husband. Lenny was having some hard times of his own. He felt he was living Mike's life in Mike's surroundings with Mike's family. I understood, but there wasn't much I could do. I noticed that things were changing, but I couldn't alter anything. This was my life, and I needed my family.

It was time for Kyle to have foot surgery (bilateral heel cord releases). It had been eight months since his last surgery, but I felt like it was yesterday. His muscle tone had improved a little, but he still had a ways to go. We were hoping that with this surgery his feet could be normal again. Maybe he could wear shoes and stand and try to strengthen his muscles. This could take up to a year or so, but that was what we were hoping for. Lenny came with Kyle and me. It was so nice having my partner with me and not being alone. It helped me so much. Making friends and seeing the same nurses and staff made it a little easier, and I knew we were in good hands. Off I went to the surgical room with Kyle until he fell asleep. Once again, I left in tears, hoping the surgery would work, wondering what it could mean for the future.

Dr. Shapiro came to tell us that the surgery had gone well. Kyle was going to be in a cast for a while, and when both legs had healed enough, they would remove the cast and put AFOs (foot braces) on. Everything sounded great. I stayed with Kyle a few days at the hospital until we were able to go home. It was so nice to see Kyle feet in a upright position. Dr. Shapiro did an incredible surgery, and what an amazing doctor he is. After a few weeks of being home and having his pain under control, Kyle went back to school.

My hand splints were finally removed. My hand still hurt, but the movement in my fingers was improving every day. Lifting my arm high was a challenge, but it was coming along. My back had been my bigger problem. Going through another surgery with Kyle and taking care of him had done my back in. I had been going for therapy, but while I was there, the therapist had shifted my back the wrong way, and now I could barely walk. The pain was so severe I couldn't even stand.

I went to my primary doctor, Dr. William Dunn and he sent me to Dr. McGillicuddy, who decided to operate the next day. After the surgery, I immediately felt relief. It was amazing. I was told that I had many problems with my back and that I shouldn't be lifting Kyle and taking those long rides to visit him three times a week. My back just couldn't take it, and I needed to stay off my feet for a few weeks to heal. That was difficult for me to hear and accept, but I knew that, for know, I had no choice. I had to heal.

Life at home was really difficult. Kyle was at school, trying to get stronger every day, trying to meet his therapy goals. The girls had school, homework, and dance, and it was hard to help them, being stuck in bed. Family chipped in to help, as usual, and Lenny was very stressed, feeling like he was a nurse. It was overwhelming for him, feeling frustrated. I told him I understood. I had a very hard life, and there wasn't much fun to be had, but I could only do what I could do. Right then, I had to focus on getting better.

I told Lenny I loved him, but I understood if he couldn't handle the situation. He was overwhelmed and hated seeing me in pain. He was very emotional and said he loved me and didn't want to lose me, but he knew it was going to be a very long road medically for both Kyle and me. Over the next couple of weeks, we all got stronger and better, and life was as normal as it could be.

Months passed, and Kyle was in AFOs. Finally, after two years, we could put sneakers on him. We put him in a stander at school, and he was petrified and cried out. It took a while, but eventually he was in a stander, not bearing much weight. It took months for him to adjust, and eventually we got a stander for home and used it on the weekends. Over time, his legs seemed to be getting stronger, but his muscle tone was still very high.

Lenny and I got engaged. We had been together for a year and decided that the big day would be in six months. Both sides of the family were shocked. I loved Lenny and knew that he loved me, and I wanted that family unit badly. He was my best friend, and I didn't want to be without him. I knew we had some hurdles because life was so difficult, but I also knew that we loved each other.

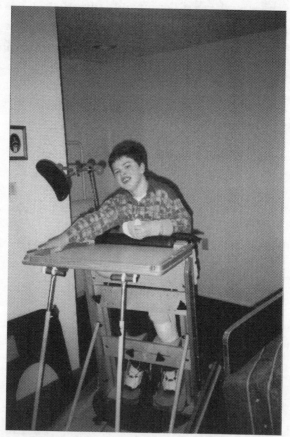

Kyle relearning how to stand and put weight on his legs again after two years

Chapter 25

The day had come. Would my children and I see justice? Regardless, we couldn't change what had happened, and I couldn't bring my husband back or give my son a normal life. What would I consider justice for the man who had caused the accident? Even a death sentence would have no meaning for me. It would be an easy way out. I thought that putting him away for a long time to think about what he had done, taking away his freedom, was more of a punishment, in a way. Then again, if it was a death sentence, this man couldn't hurt anyone ever again. Of course, we were not looking at a death sentence, but I couldn't help thinking about it. This man had destroyed our lives. He had taken so much from my children and me, and he hadn't really been hurt physically. Was he hurt emotionally?

My children and I arrived at the courthouse. Kyle was anxious and furious. He had so much he wanted to tell Keith Doucette. Laying eyes on Keith for the first time, my girls looked scared but brave as the man was brought in handcuffs and chains. They asked, "Mommy, is that who killed Daddy?" With tears in my eyes, I said, "Yes, that's him."

Kyle put up his middle finger to show his emotions. I told Kyle it was okay and tried to relax him. His muscle tone was high, and he was having spasms. As we sat there, I was called out of the courtroom and told by the district attorney that Keith had decided to plead guilty. "What does that mean?" I asked.

"By his pleading guilty, we don't have to have a trial. The judge is going to sentence him today, and it will be over."

Be over? I was in shock, as I had prepared myself for a trial. The district attorney explained to me that by pleading guilty to manslaughter, the vehicular homicide charge would be dismissed. I was not happy. How did pleading guilty take away the fact that he had killed my husband and severely hurt my family? But it was the way the court system worked, and I had no say about it. We were only the victims!

The district attorney told me to take some time to go into a quiet room where I could write up a victim's statement, and off I went. I was so angry, but I knew I had to write, and write fast. It took me about an hour to write a three-page statement.

When I walked back into the courtroom, I sat near my family and children. The girls held my hand, not understanding what was going to happen. Keith and his attorney were sitting on one side of the room, and the district attorney was on the other side. Everyone stood, and Judge Daniel F. Toomey walked in. When he was seated, everyone else sat down.

The judge asked Keith how he chose to plead. Keith said, "Guilty." The judge asked him and his attorney if everything had been explained to him and if he understood the charges. Keith replied, "Yes." The judge asked if any victim statements were going to be read, and the district attorney said yes.

The judge said I could go up to the front. I got up out of my seat, trying to stay strong, shaking and in tears. I walked by Keith, arrived at the podium, and looked at the judge, who told me to begin.

Looking right at Keith, I began to tell him what a wonderful and caring husband and father he had taken from us. I let him know that Mike had adopted Kyle and Kyle had looked up to Mike, especially since he had a father who didn't want any part in his life. Mike had given Kyle love, affection, and time, something he had needed so badly in his young life, and now Keith had taken that from him. My young girls did not have their daddy, and they cried at night, not understanding why their daddy had had to die. Kyle was trying to grieve, but he couldn't because of his condition. All his fears and emotions were now held inside. Communicating was a great challenge for him, and it was very difficult for him to express his feelings. He no longer even had tears.

I told Keith that Kyle had been athletic and smart, and I listed all the sports and things that Kyle could no longer do. Everyday things—like getting dressed, cleaning himself, feeding himself, and doing everything we all take for granted—Kyle could no longer do. I told Keith to think about not being able to move or reposition himself in bed or even scratch a simple itch. Kyle was paralyzed now, dependent on others for everything. Now his life was full of medical needs, many surgeries, and discomfort from spasms. He was adjusting to his sisters taking care of him now. He had gone from being a happy child full of life to being trapped within his own body. Traumatic brain injury and two strokes later, he still managed a smile and was determined to survive.

I described Kimberly's speech problems and anxiety, her wanting me home when I couldn't be, thinking I loved Kyle more. At only six years of age, how was she supposed to understand all of this? I talked about Katie and how she'd had to relearn how to walk after being in a body cast for two months, screaming from pain and spasms, asking when her brother would be able to play with her again. I said that it was difficult raising children so young without their daddy, whom they loved so much.

I talked about myself and said that I was just regaining the use of my arm after three surgeries while trying to adjust to our new life. Being in hospitals for seven and a half months before coming home had been very hard on all of us. I said that I missed my best friend so much and that I was trying to figure out how to survive.

I said that I had asked Kyle if he wanted to tell Keith anything, and Kyle had said, "Yes. Don't drink and drive." That came from an eleven-year-old boy, whose life Keith had changed forever.

When I was finished, Norman, my brother-in-law, who had been a police officer at the time, told about arriving at the scene of the accident and seeing his two nieces lying in the middle of route 20. Then he'd had to tell his mother that she had lost her son to a drunk driver. He told the judge about Keith's long history of speeding violations and said that his license had been scheduled to be suspended—the week after the accident occurred.

Before imposing the sentence, Judge Toomey said, "There is no sentence that I or anyone can impose that would restore the Brodeur family to what it was before the defendant's criminal acts." Then he sentenced Keith to three to five years in state prison, with ten years' probation to begin after his release. Conditions of probation included drug and alcohol evaluation and one hundred hours of community service a year. Keith was also ordered not to drive a car for seven years after he got out.

Keith apologized, saying, "I'm very sorry for what happened. I wish I could take that day back."

As they took Keith away, I was shaking and crying, but I saw nothing from him. I asked myself, *does he even really care about what he did? Does he have emotions? How could he not show any feelings when he was being taken away, knowing he was being put away for a few years?* I tried to make sense of it then, and even to this day, I can't.

After Keith was gone, I was introduced to his probation officer, Geraldo Alicea. He informed me that he would be keeping in touch with Mr. Doucette when he was released from prison. He would make sure that Keith was doing what the court had ordered, as far as his probation and having drug testing done. He told me he would be in touch with me if there were any issues. I felt very confident in Mr. Alicea, and I knew he would make sure Mr. Doucette was complying with his court order.

Three years went by so fast, as my children and I were still healing and trying to make the best of our lives. Kyle had more surgeries, and I wondered when they would come to an end for him. Keith was coming up for parole, which didn't seem fair, but I knew there wasn't much we could do about it.

My children and I and our immediate family members went to Boston for Keith's parole hearing. Keith went before a panel of three judges, where his attorneys and the district attorney argued their cases.

Keith's attorney wanted him to be set free. He stated that his client had been on good behavior while in prison and that he felt bad about what he had done to the Brodeur family. He asked for an early release date. The district attorney stated that Keith should serve the maximum sentence because Michael had died and Kyle was still in hospitals and having surgeries. He pleaded his case very well.

I looked at Keith and still saw no reaction. He just stared straight ahead. I still couldn't figure him out. He looked like a very cold person with no heart. I thought I would hate to be him. Leaving the court that day, everyone felt that there was no way that the judges would release him and that he would definitely serve the remainder of his time, minus the time for good behavior. Months later, we were told that he would stay in prison for his remaining sentence. I felt relieved, but I realized that he would soon be free, and I worried about the future. Would he make good choices? Would he hurt another family? The only good thing was we knew that he couldn't drive for seven years, and that he would be on probation and watched closely for ten years.

I was notified when Keith was released, and I heard that he left the area. I was happy about that. We both lived in Charlton, Massachusetts, only ten minutes from each other, and I didn't want to run into him. I tried not to think of him much, as my energy went into my kids. But believe me, when I was at Children's Hospital with Kyle being cut open again and again, I couldn't help but think of him and be angry that he had chosen to drink and drive that night. Still, I knew I couldn't focus on him. Praying and talking to Mike was my comfort, and I had to believe and have hope to get through my days.

Chapter 26

It was a beautiful day in May, and the weather was perfect on the day I got married. The kids were full of excitement—the girls in their beautiful dresses and Kyle so handsome in his tuxedo. As I put on my long, white, fitted dress, I felt excited, but I also couldn't believe I was getting married and Mike wasn't here. I sat on the side of the bed that morning, talking to Mike and letting him know how much I would always love and adore him, saying that no matter what I did in life, I would never forget him.

I could hear all my bridesmaids downstairs getting ready. My parents arrived, with the photographer right behind them. They yelled for me to come down. Taking family pictures with all three girls and Kyle was so sweet. I was feeling so blessed to have all my children, and now I had another daughter to love. I was so happy that Cassie was part of my life.

Heading to Notre Dame Church, I was excited to see Lenny, but I was nervous to go down the aisle. The music was playing, and my flower girls, Kimberly and Katie, went down the aisle, so cute and smiling. Cassie, my junior bridesmaid looked so gorgeous and was smiling at her father. My bridesmaids and maid of honor looked radiant.

Then it was my turn. I held my father's arm and looked straight ahead at Lenny and Kyle. I walked down the aisle in tears, with waves of emotion going through me. I was so happy to be with Lenny, but I felt bad that I had lost my husband. Once I reached Lenny, I felt good.

I felt safe and secure, and I knew we loved each other. Saying our vows meant so much to me. We had a beautiful mass, and before I knew it, it was over. We were a family, our children excited that they are brother and sisters. Off we went to our reception at the Ramada Inn in Auburn, Massachusetts.

Family and friends wished us well, but the wedding was also hard on a lot of people. They were thinking of Mike, thinking that this shouldn't be happening. Why had we all had to lose Mike? It was a day of trying to move on in life, but it was also a reminder of someone who was loved very much, someone who shouldn't have died.

We took a cruise for our honeymoon. It was very relaxing and something I needed badly. It was a break from hospitals and appointments. It was what life was all about, and we just took it all in. The food and entertainment were great. I gained eleven pounds that week, and it was my first time having a week alone with Lenny—and no kids. Neither of us wanted it to end. It was nice to have fun and to feel loved. It was a honeymoon I will never forget.

When we returned to reality, the kids were happy we were back, and they were full of stories. I went back to my normal routine, going to Massachusetts Hospital School to visit Kyle three times a week. The girls were getting ready for a dance recital, and another school year was coming to an end.

Lenny's dream was to build a house in Charlton near his parents, so we drew up some plans and got a builder. The house would be completely handicap accessible for Kyle, from ramps to lifts, with extra-wide doorways and hallways. Kyle was in a motorized chair now, and he needed a lot of room, as he had difficulty driving it, especially with his left-side neglect. He had trouble turning his neck to the left side.

It was exciting to think about owning my own home, but it was sad to know that I would have to leave my family that I lived next to for eleven years. It was going to be a big adjustment. I wouldn't have Aunt Jean helping me any longer, so I would need to hire a personal care attendant. Jean and I had worked so well together. She is the best sister-in-law I could have asked for. I loved having Rita, Jean, Ronald, and Gloria next door to me. I had seen them every day. But I knew it was important for Lenny to have his own surroundings and a place that was his, not Mike's.

One night while Lenny and I were sound asleep in bed, I had a dream that seemed very real. Mike came to me and told me that everything was going to be okay and that I shouldn't worry. He had wings that were flapping, and he was all dressed in white. I could only see him from the waist up, but he looked just like Mike. I awoke and sat up instantly, reaching out for him. Mike flew away as I cried, "Please don't go! Don't go!" My crying woke Lenny, and I told him about my dream. He didn't say too much. He just held me and went back to sleep.

In the morning, I told everyone what had happened in my dream, because it had been so real. Mike coming to me that night meant so much to me, because leaving his family and my surroundings was really hard. I knew that his mother would miss the kids, and I was just worried about everything. I didn't want to hurt anyone, especially Rita. I loved her so much, but I also knew that we were only fifteen minutes away, and we could come visit.

When I told Rita about my dream, she was in tears. This wasn't the first time this had happened. Shortly after the accident, I had received a phone call from a woman in California, who told me that she had been praying for a Lisa she didn't know—until her daughter told her about our accident. I was shocked that she had called to tell me this. She had me in tears, telling me that Mike loved me and needed me to stay strong. She said that I would get through this and that Mike would never leave me; he loved his young children and me too much. The woman reminded me to pray and to talk to Mike, as he was always listening. I have to say that, since the first day of our accident, I had already been doing what she told me. When she called and told me these things, I knew she was correct, because I felt Mike spirit with me and his guidance.

A year after that, she called again. At the time, I was experiencing survivor's guilt. I had been trying to go on with my life, but I was missing Mike badly, wanting to understand why I had survived instead of him. When she called, she said that Mike had asked her to call to deliver a message from him. I was in tears immediately. She said, "Mike doesn't want you to feel guilty. It's okay to move on. He knows how much you love him, but you need to do what's right for you."

I couldn't believe I had received a message like this. I hadn't told anyone how I was feeling. It made me feel so much better. When I told Rita about my survivor's guilt, she said, "Lisa, don't feel bad. Mike would never have been able to handle all of this. With Kyle being so injured and everything the girls have been through, Mike would have been a miserable person. He would have gone after Keith, and then he would have been put away. Believe me, if only one of you could live, he would have wanted you to live." Talking to my mother-in-law had always helped me. She was a very wise woman and had been through so much in life. I really valued her approval and opinion.

One afternoon, the phone rang. When I answered it, a woman on the line said, "Lisa, this is Cheryl. I wanted to let you know that Kyle has a little sister named Breanna. I had her a few weeks ago." In shock, I congratulated her. Then she informed me that she was not with Kyle Sr., the baby's father. He didn't see their daughter, but she wanted Breanna to grow up with her brother. I was happy for Kyle to have a baby sister, so I said yes, of course, she could come to see him anytime.

Cheryl came the following week. Brianna was gorgeous and small. Kyle smiled as he held her in his wheelchair, so proud to know that this was his baby sister. My little girls were confused. Kyle had a sister? I explained that Kyle had had another daddy who didn't see him, and that there daddy Michael had adopted Kyle and had given him the last name Brodeur. They said, "Okay, but Kyle's *our* brother," and I said, "Yes, he is!" They loved it when Breanna came over, as she was like a little doll to them. They loved being little mommies, and Cheryl was always so good with them—and especially with Kyle. This was a blessing in our lives, and I was so happy that Kyle and Breanna would grow up having each other.

Chapter 27

Driving to our new house in the country, we saw cows and ducks along our road. The kids were very excited to have a new home. To them, it was huge, and they always said, "We can get lost in this house!" I laughed and said, "You'll get used to it."

Moving in was a lot of work. I had gone through all of Mike's stuff in the attic. He had so much, but I couldn't part with it, so it all came into our new home. I gave away the clothing he hadn't worn, but I kept most of it and put it in bags in the attic. Going through some paperwork in my bedroom, I came across Mike's wallet from the night of the accident. Looking through it, I found receipts from his trip to England and pictures of all of us. It brought me to tears. I still couldn't believe he wasn't coming back. Suddenly something inside me said, *Go into the kitchen.* Holding Mike's wallet, I went. I looked up at the balcony and saw a shadow of Mike walking upstairs. It happened so fast. I yelled, "Mike, I hope you like it." It made me feel so good to know he was checking on us. I'd had a few visuals of him by then, so I was getting use to it.

Lenny loved his new home, and being a man, he loved his finished basement, his man cave. Lenny spent a lot of time down there, while I preferred to be upstairs, because the kids were young, and I needed to be where they were. Decorating the house was a lot of fun. Lenny's mom, Ginny, helped me so much. We got it all done in two days. Ginny was a sweet and beautiful woman, inside and out. I loved being around her and my father-in-law Lenny Sr. He is a sweet man also, and I loved talking to him. He is a very easygoing person, and we all got along great.

Kyle was having a lot of pain in his hip. We had fixed his feet (bilateral heel cord releases) this past year. While Kyle was in casting, his muscle tone had shifted to his right hip. Dr. Shapiro had some X-rays taken and informed us that Kyle would need a hip replacement in the future. I was in shock. He was only thirteen years old! We did the best we could to manage his pain and would hold off as long as we could.

Kyle's spine was curving more. The body jacket helped but couldn't correct it. His muscle tone was taking over his body. I knew my son's future was going to be one of pain and suffering, but I had to hope for the best and hope for some medical breakthrough that would help Kyle.

Kyle always handled everything very well. Amazingly, he always kept his sense of humor. When Kyle survived the accident, I knew our lives were going to be a tough and bumpy roller coaster ride with many sharp curves—, which was exactly what we'd had so far. I always said, "Let's take one day at a time. Deep breathes. We will deal with it as it comes, and when you can't take the pain and the time is right, we will fix your hip." Kyle agreed, knowing we would take action when he was ready, and he gave me a thumb up.

We didn't talk about his spine much. I figured we would focus on the hip first. Besides, a spinal fusion scared the living daylights out of me. We still went to Boston every month to increase his Baclofen pump, and every three months for a pump refill. Kyle and I felt like Children's Hospital was our second home; we were there so much. When we left there, we always bought a special treat to eat on the way home. It was the best part of the trip.

Kyle had graduated from pureed foods and was eating small, diced meats. The easiest way to get meats into Kyle was to put them in mashed potatoes or some other soft food to help him swallow it. At home, my mother, Aunt Jean, and I had made all his food. When he started school, he tried their food, but we noticed he was losing weight, and Kyle was so tiny already that it wasn't good. Kyle said he didn't like the food at school, so we all made meals and kept them frozen. I packed nine meals a week as well as breakfast food. He loved it and started to gain weight again. I loved knowing that he was having home-cooked meals and food he loved.

It took Kyle two years to sip from a straw, which was a huge step. I hoped that in time he would develop stronger sucking power so he could have a shake. He gained his full smile back and could stick out his tongue farther. His impulsivity wasn't as bad, but it was still noticeable. Kyle was very smart. His math skills were remarkable, and he could add, subtract, multiply, and do a little division. He couldn't speak well. It was like a baby learning. He had trouble getting the air to form sound, and he spelled everything out. We had to have a lot of patience. Using pictures helped a lot.

Spending so much time with Kyle, we all just learned what he wanted. We noticed that when we put him to bed, he had more air for his voice while he was lying down. It was so much easier to communicate with him. Kyle had it very tough, but he always put a smile on. Together as a family, we stayed optimistic, and I always told him, "There is no such word as *no* or *can't*. We will find ways."

As a family, we went together to movies, restaurants, shopping, and even the beach. It was very tough at times. Sometimes when we were out somewhere, Kyle would be in so much pain that we would have to leave and take our food with us, or leave in the middle of a movie. It was tough to hear my child crying out in pain and know there was not much I could do for him. All I could do was leave and get him home and into bed.

The girls would try to change his mind and put cold towels on him to wipe away his sweat. In the car, we would move his legs and rub them, and sometimes he would cry all the way home. It wasn't a normal cry, as he didn't have tears. These were cries of pain that went right through me, making me feel helpless, and I couldn't get home fast enough. Taking care of Kyle was not a one-person task; it took all of us as a family. All three of my girls were my biggest helpers, especially spending time with him and making him laugh. They were Kyle's best medicine.

Months went by, and the pain in Kyle's hip was getting worse. When he couldn't take it any longer, we decided to do his hip replacement right after the holidays. The holidays came and went by so fast. Everyone had a good time and loved all the gifts—and especially the one in memory of their father. That year it was a picture of them with their father. The photo was blown up into a cardboard cutout that stood up like a trophy. They displayed the picture in their room so they could see it every day, showing it to everyone who came over. The kids were happy, but we were dreading the weeks ahead.

It was time for another surgery, and Lenny and I took Kyle to the hospital. Kyle seemed to just want to get it done. I always tried to be happy and not let Kyle see my fear. While he was waiting to go in, I made him laugh by telling him that I was going to tell the doctor that he was ready to have his sex change. Kyle laughed and said, "Yeah, do it!" Lenny was very serious, saying, "You'd better not. That's embarrassing."

When the anesthesiologist arrived, he asked, "What is Kyle having done today?" I said, "He's ready for his sex change. He can't wait to be a girl." Kyle laughed loudly, and the anesthesiologist was speechless. The nurse laughed and said, "Kyle, I'll get you a pink robe." Lenny shook his head, in shock that I'd said it. We were the only ones laughing in pre-op. Kyle kept laughing, and we carried the joke into the operating room until he was asleep. I thanked them all for being such good sports. In tears, I left Kyle, saying, "Please take good care of him."

Lenny had waited for me in the waiting room with Kyle's wheelchair and personal belongings, seeing all the parents waiting anxiously for their children to be out of surgery. It was a different world at Children's Hospital, with lots of sadness. People from all over the world were trying to go to the best place for their child, hoping that God would work miracles through these doctors' hands. I was so thankful to the wonderful doctors and nurses that I'd had the pleasure of knowing. They were all so kind and considerate and helped in any way they could.

The surgery took multiple hours, and when Dr. Shapiro came, he said it was a success. The bad news involved two things. First, Kyle's right leg would not grow as fast as his left leg, so now he would have uneven legs. I thought that would be okay, because I knew Kyle didn't have any chance of walking, and he couldn't stand in his prone stander any longer. Second, he would have to be in a body cast from head to toe for three long months. Three months! How was he going to handle that? The purpose of that was to keep him from moving. His muscle tone was so strong that they'd had no choice but to do a body cast.

We chose to put him in a blue cast, as it was Kyle's favorite color. I was concerned about how I was going to change him, because he couldn't wear a diaper. They put a hole in the cast for hygiene and told us to use thick pads with plastic around the edges so the cast wouldn't get wet. A body cast meant that Kyle could not get out of bed. He would be stuck in a lying-down position. I couldn't believe that two of my children had had to be in body casts! Katie had only been three years old and much smaller. Kyle was heavier, and his situation would be much harder.

Kyle woke up in his body cast, his new home for the next three months, and so far he was not complaining. We stayed in the hospital to make sure there were no fevers or infections from the new hardware that had been put in. We tried to get his pain under control. It was a big adjustment for Kyle not to be wearing his body jacket, which he normally wore all day long. I was worried that we were going to lose his spine position even more. But there wasn't anything we could do. We had no choice. All I knew was that this was going to be a long three months.

I called the girls to let them know that Kyle was doing okay. I told them about the body cast, and they couldn't wait to sign it. They always hated it when I had to leave and Kyle was having surgery, as they worried a lot. They knew that his surgeries were not simple ones, and they always involved long recoveries. I always tried to reassure them that everything was going to be okay and that we would be home before they knew it.

We were able to go home after a week. I didn't send Kyle to his program at the hospital school, as I wanted him to recover at home. Being on so much medicine, Kyle got a bacterial infection called *Clostridium difficile*, or *C. diff.* I called his pediatrician, Dr. Giordano who made a house call for us. After that, he came every week or so, as needed, to check on Kyle. I was very blessed to have such a wonderful and caring doctor. As the weeks went by and Kyle was adjusting to his body cast, he was feverish on and off. The *C. diff* was just awful, but we maintained great hygiene, and overall we kept the cast very clean.

Worried about his low-grade fevers, we went in for a checkup, where we removed his body cast to look at the incision. The incision was infected, which required another surgery to clean it out. We just could not catch a break. We put a cast back on him, but this time it was a removable shell. We were able to remove the top part to wash his skin and then put it back on, nice and tight, with long, white straps.

We received a date to clean out the incision later that week. It was a fast surgery, and again Kyle handled everything okay. We stayed a few days and then went home. Mellissa Miller a nurse came to my house to show me how to pack his wound. The wound had to heal from the inside out, and I packed it every few days until it was healed weeks later. Katie loved wounds and loved helping me take care of it. Kim wasn't into wounds, but she watched.

As the last two months went by slowly, Kyle and I anxiously waited for the day the cast would come off. At the doctor's office, we waited for the X-rays. Then Dr. Shapiro came in and said that everything looked good and that his cast could come off. Kyle was so excited at the prospect of sitting up, free from a cast that had encased him for so long. As he lay on the table, I held his hand and undid the straps of the cast. Kyle's eyes got big, as he feared what was ahead. I told him it was okay and talked to him in positive terms, reminding him that he would be able to put clothes on—including his Michael Jordan sneakers!

Rolling Kyle's body out of the cast, we washed him down. His skin was very chafed and dry, and we rubbed lotion on his tiny legs. After packing his wound every other day, I could see that the incision and infection site were healing well from the inside out. Everything was coming along. Now we had to get Kyle back to a sitting position in his wheelchair, and he would have to learn to tolerate his body jacket once again. It was a slow process, during which I realized that his spine had gotten worse while he was in the body cast. That meant that his jacket needed to be altered for his new curvature.

Overall, Kyle recovered well from this major surgery. I asked him if he would like to go to Walt Disney World the day after Christmas. His thumb went up fast, and he smiled. I knew it was still a ways off, but it gave him something big to look forward to. We made it a surprise, and he didn't tell his sisters.

Chapter 28

Christmas was near, and the kids were excited about the holidays, wondering what Santa would bring them and what Daddy's gift would be this year. I had started a tradition that the kids loved: I love talking to them about their daddy and reminding them how much he loved them. We often watched family videos, and it was healthy for us all. It was so important to me that my children felt their daddy's love.

I had started some other traditions during the year as well. For Father's Day and for their daddy's birthday, we always went to the cemetery with helium balloons. Kyle's was blue, Kim's was yellow, Katie's was pink, and mine was red. We all wrote messages and attached them to the balloons. Then we said a special prayer and sent the balloons off. The kids loved it and felt like they could still give their father something, only in a different way. It was priceless, when the balloons took off, to see the excitement in the kids' faces, full of hope that Daddy would receive their messages and love the pictures they'd drawn for him. I know Mike was looking down with a big smile.

For almost a year, Kyle had kept an important secret from his sisters: that we were all going to Walt Disney World in Florida. On Christmas morning, the girls would find out that we were leaving the next day. Kyle was excited but nervous about flying, worried about having spasms. I kept trying to tell Kyle he would be fine, that we would make sure he was comfortable.

Christmas morning came, and the children woke up to luggage, Disney items, and clothes for their vacation. Then Lenny and I told them we were leaving for Disney World the next day. The girls jumped up and down, looking at each other in shock. It was a busy but fun day, and even Kyle was getting excited.

Morning came, and there was a lot of luggage, especially for Kyle. We had to bring a wedge for sleeping, and I'd ordered a hospital bed for our room at the resort. We gathered diapers, wipes, medicine, clothes, a brace, snacks, and special food to take medicine. There was so much to carry, but we did it. The girls were great at handling their own stuff.

Going through the X-ray machine was not easy with Kyle. Security staff felt him all over, and we had to take his shoes off and pick him up out of the chair so they could check his seat cushion. I couldn't believe how much work it was. Kyle was unhappy and in pain from all the moving around. Thank God that Lenny could lift him. It's complicated to move someone who can't do anything for himself if you can't lift him. We were relieved when we got the okay to move on.

Arriving at the desk where we would board the airplane, I told the stewardess that Kyle couldn't walk. We had a wheelchair that needed to go below the plane after we carried Kyle on board. The staff was very good, and Lenny carried Kyle onto the plane. He set Kyle onto a seat, trying to keep his body in an upright position, and used straps to hold him in. Unfortunately, Kyle's neck was hanging down. Lenny sat next to Kyle, trying to hold his head up with a neck pillow, but Kyle didn't like it. Kyle was not happy at all, as he couldn't sit upright. His body didn't allow him to. We just needed to get into the air. Once we were at a safe flight level, we laid Kyle down on top of us. He seemed to like that much better. The flight was three hours long, and I was very happy when we landed. The girls couldn't wait to arrive at Disney World.

People got off the plane, staring as they walked by us. I assume they were amazed, wondering how we'd flown with Kyle and feeling bad for him. We were the last ones off the plane, and the attendants got Kyle's wheelchair. Lenny carried Kyle out, and once Kyle was seated in his wheelchair, he looked relieved. We'd done it! We were in Florida!

Our hotel was beautiful, and everything there was great. There was transportation at every bus stop. I was so happy that our first vacation together was going so well. We were all amazed by our surroundings. We especially loved the magical parade, the light shows, the character breakfast, and the rides.

One night the kids wanted to go to Lego Land. Lenny didn't want to go, so he stayed behind at the hotel. The kids and I went, and while we were there, I had a problem with Kyle's wheelchair. The wheel came off! What was I to do? I had a six-, eight-, and eleven-year-old, and Kyle's chair had only one wheel. I couldn't roll him anywhere, because his chair was stuck in one spot. I wouldn't let the girls leave me to get help, because it was getting dark out, and I didn't want to lose them.

We stayed put until someone came by, and then we asked for help. It took about three hours to find someone who could put a wheel on his wheelchair. Once we'd found someone, he had to take the wheel from us. We had to hold Kyle up in his wheelchair with only one wheel. It was quite a project, and we all kept taking turns, but it was hard, as Kyle was heavy. It was a very interesting night, and the girls were so good and helpful, but I was so happy to get back to our hotel room that night.

Our week went by fast. On our last night, we saw a huge fireworks show for New Year's Day. It was beautiful, and the lit-up sky looked magical. In the morning, we were all packed and ready to go to the airport. This time, knowing what was ahead of us, we were more prepared. Going through the X-ray was easier this time, as they let us go through without taking Kyle out of his chair. Boarding the plane went well also, and there were a lot of curious people. All of us had a magical time!

Back at home, Kimberly ran down the stairs, stumbled and fell to the bottom of the stairway, and landed on Kyle's stair lift. I went to her immediately to see if she was okay and found that her head was gushing blood. I got a towel to try to stop the bleeding but had no luck, so I had to take her to the hospital emergency room. When we arrived at the ER, the staff took her in immediately.

The doctor asked, "How did she do this?" I said, "She fell and hit my son's handicap lift." He asked what was wrong with my son. I said that he'd had a traumatic brain injury and two strokes. He asked if I'd ever heard of magnetic therapy. When I said no, he explained that a person would lie under a huge magnet for multiple hours. This helped to heal bones and repair brain cells and fractures. Amazed, I said, "Really? Repair brain cells?" The doctor felt that one particular facility could help Kyle, but the down side was that our insurance didn't cover it. I went home and immediately looked up the imaging center. It sounded great. I called them and got more information. I asked Kyle's doctors if they had ever heard of this imaging center, but they hadn't.

After researching and getting the okay from both the doctor at the imaging center and Kyle's doctor, we made plans to go. First, we had to turn off Kyle's Baclofen pump. This was scary, because we knew that Kyle could possibly have more spasms. The doctor gave me a prescription for Baclofen, but we knew that taking it by mouth didn't have much effect on Kyle, so I had Valium, just in case, to be given as needed. My brother Danny, Kimberly, Katie, Kyle, and I headed to North Carolina for two weeks. It was an eighteen-hour drive, but the girls were excited to get there, anxious to see if this could help their brother. Kyle went along with anything that might help him to get back to the way he had been. He was willing to try anything.

Arriving at the Magnetic Therapy Image Center, I was anxious to start the treatment. We saw the huge magnet and were all amazed at how big it was. Getting Kyle up the ramp to the bed was difficult. Danny lifted Kyle onto the bed, and the staff slid the bed under the magnet—only three to five inches away from his head. The magnet was so huge; it covered Kyle from his thigh to over his head.

Kyle stayed under this magnet for twelve hours at night and then got up for two hours for breakfast. He went back down for six hours and was up for four hours. We did this for two weeks. Danny stayed overnight with the girls at a hotel, and they spent the days with Kyle and me at the facility. When Kyle took his four-hour supper break, we ate and then took Kyle swimming at the hotel pool. Kyle loved the water, and even though we had to hold him, he did great. He would hold his nose, and we'd dunk him under the water.

Kyle always amazed me. Being paralyzed and so limited in movement, he was still willing to try anything. It made me think back to when I'd made him go out for the first time, telling him that we still had to live but would do things in other ways. Kyle had not been happy with me back then, but now he would try anything I'd allow him to do—and more. I was so fortunate and thankful to have my brother Danny with me to help with so much lifting. I never could have done it alone.

After a few days, we started to see Kyle loosen up. His muscle tone was not so tight, and Kyle said he felt loose. Not having spasms was a huge improvement, and I didn't have to give him any Valium. When the two weeks were over and we were ready to go home, the doctor said that we would continue to see results in the next couple of weeks. Going home had never felt better, and Kyle was happy not to be under the magnet any longer. We laughed about our adventure and hoped that Kyle would keep showing progress.

Over the next weeks, we noticed that Kyle could drive his motorized chair better. Some of his impulsiveness had diminished, but his muscle tone had increased again. To me, it was worth every penny just to have him master his motorized wheelchair. We had been trying for many months, but Kyle had had such difficulty that he had to be supervised. Now he was free to use his chair at school, full-time, on low speed with some assistance. Even at home he could drive in the house. From a distance, I watched him smile with pride that he could do it! This was a huge benefit. It gave Kyle independence, and he had freedom to go wherever he wanted without asking. I smiled with joy, just watching my son.

While we'd been at the magnet center, they had informed us about a treatment called Hyperbaric Oxygen Chamber, another treatment that was not covered by insurance. Since Kyle had had two strokes, they thought this treatment could possibly help him. I looked into it and figured we could try it in the summer. It was another big expense, but the chamber doctor said it couldn't hurt Kyle, and other people with brain injuries were having great success with it, so I figured we would try it.

Kyle said he was willing, so off we went on a two-hour drive to Great Barrington. The chamber was a huge tank like a submarine, and Kyle lay down in it while wearing a headpiece. They called it a *dive*, and it was very interesting, but Kyle ended up getting ear infections, so we never got to find out if it would have worked for him.

It was early morning, around five a.m., and everyone was sleeping, when I heard a big bang and Kyle cried out. I jumped out of bed and ran to Kyle's room to find him on the floor! Lenny lifted him back up to bed. I wondered how he had flipped himself over the bars of his hospital bed. I checked him out, shocked that he was not hurt, and asked him, "How did you flip yourself over with one arm?"

Kyle said clearly in a deep voice, "I was having a dream that I could walk!" I was shocked and told him he was lucky he hadn't been hurt. I felt so bad for him, knowing how much he wanted to be able to walk and do things for himself. Kissing him good-night, I said, "Go back to sleep. And no more flipping yourself out of bed!"

Kyle undergoing magnetic therapy in North Carolina with his sisters

Chapter 29

It was early on a dark and rainy morning on our way to Children's Hospital, and I was thinking about what a miserable day it was. Kyle was sound asleep, knowing that a huge surgery was only hours away. He was scared, but he knew there was no way around it. It had to be done.

It seemed only yesterday that Dr. Shapiro had told me that Kyle's spine was curving. Over the years, we had put him in several body jackets, making new ones as Kyle outgrew them. I had been told that he would need a spinal fusion in a few years, and now the time we'd been dreading had come. Kyle was only fourteen now and was still growing. We were told that if Kyle didn't have the surgery, he would suffer a long and painful death, as his organs would crush together. I went and received another opinion, and Dr. McGillicuddy said the same thing. There was no other choice. While talking to Dr. McGillicuddy I thanked him for saving Kyle's life, telling him how far Kyle has come, and that he had his mind, long and short-term memory. The doctor was amazed that Kyle even survived. I hung up the phone thinking what an amazing doctor he is, and what a miracle I was given.

When I'd left those appointments with Kyle, I had tried to be strong and positive to keep him from being frightened, but this surgery was different for him. He was scared and didn't want it. He said, "Let me die." I explained that I couldn't put him through that, as it would be a long, painful death. I told him we had to do it and that I would help him. I was petrified of this surgery myself and cried much over it. It was one of the worst surgeries a person could have. The best part was that there would be no more body jacket. Kyle was even frightened of that. All he knew was his jacket, which was tight on him. He no longer knew what it was like just to wear a simple shirt.

When we arrived at Children's Hospital, there were very few cars in valet parking. I unloaded Kyle from the car. He didn't want to go in and said no. It was breaking my heart, and I was in tears as I tried to tell him that we had no choice. As we entered the hospital, I took a deep breath, stopped to give Kyle a hug, and told him he would be okay. "You are so tough and have come so far," I said. "We can't give up now. We can do this!"

Kyle said, "I am tough," and off we went to the elevators to go to pre-op.

We got Kyle into a hospital bed, where he clutched his brown, stuffed bear and a picture of his daddy and him. Dr. Shapiro and an anesthesiologist came in to talk about the surgery. They were very serious but very nice. They asked Kyle what flavor mask he wanted, and he said he wanted lemonade. Kyle always requested lemonade, because his daddy had loved it, and he thought it was good luck. Then, off we went, down the hall to the operating room. We got him settled on the table, and I held his hand until he was asleep. As I got ready to leave, my strength weakened, and I broke down in tears, knowing what was ahead of my little boy once again.

I was told that the surgery would take all day, and it was only 8:30 a.m. Lenny was with me. We went to sit down in the waiting room, and I tried to get myself together as we waited for updates. Breakfast, lunch, and dinner came and went. We were told that the surgery was going well, but we still had a couple more hours to go. Other parents who had come in the morning had been gone for hours now, and Lenny and I were the only ones left. I was nervous and sick to my stomach.

Dr. Shapiro came out, looking relieved that the surgery was done. He told us that Kyle was being closed up, and he explained what he had done. He had tried to straighten out Kyle's spine as much as he could. He had a Posterior Spinal Fusion from the pelvis to below the neck.

Dr. Shapiro put in two steel rods the thickness of a pinky finger on each side of his spine, and wrapped it all with wire, all the way down his back. Kyle had lost so much blood that he'd had to receive multiple transfusions, but he was doing well and was stable. We were told that Kyle would have to stay on a ventilator for the next twelve to twenty-four hours. He would be taken to the intensive care unit to be watched closely, and if everything went well and he was breathing on his own, they could take out the ventilator. It was a lot to take in.

Seeing Kyle with a ventilator brought back so many memories of when the accident had first happened four years earlier. I held his hand and talked to him, telling him he'd done great and that he was the toughest kid around. I let him know how proud his father was of him. The nurse wanted Kyle to stay calm and quiet to get some rest. It was late at night by then, so Lenny left. The nurse showed me a place across the hall where I could lie down, and she said they would come to get me if there were any changes.

When I hit that bed, I felt relieved, but I knew we weren't out of danger yet. Kyle had to wake up and breathe on his own. I wondered if he would be angry at me. Would he be able to handle the pain? So many things went through my mind. In tears, I thought about everything he had gone through. I talked to Mike and asked him to please watch over our little boy. I thought positively about how far we had come together as a family. We would survive this also. I said one more prayer, thanking Jesus for guiding Dr. Shapiro through a very difficult surgery and praying that Kyle would not be in a lot of pain. I also asked Jesus to give me the strength I needed to take care of Kyle. My eyes feeling so heavy, I fell asleep.

When morning arrived, Kyle was doing well, and his medicine was tapering off. Kyle was aware of the ventilator, and he was angry. He wanted it out of his mouth. I told him we couldn't remove it just yet, that we needed to wait a little longer until he was breathing on his own. Early afternoon came, and Dr. Shapiro checked on him, getting good results. He said the ventilator could come out. Kyle put his thumb up, happy that they were going to pull it out. He lowered his head and gagged a little as the nurse pulled out the tube. It was done!

I was thrilled and excited to have the ventilator out, but I was worried. What was Kyle going to say? Was the pain going to be so bad that he would be mad at me? Kyle looked relieved and tried to say something, but I couldn't make it out. I got his spelling chart, and he spelled out, "Thank you. I'm not in so much pain!" With tears of relief, I said, "Not in pain? They said this surgery was one of the worst a person could have, and you're in less pain now?" It didn't make sense, but I was glad to take it. Kyle was different anyway, always surprising the doctors.

In the morning, we were put in a regular hospital room. Kyle was doing great and even eating. Dr. Shapiro came in and couldn't believe that Kyle was doing so well. I knew we wouldn't be there for two weeks. We had to stay for a few days, and then Dr. Shapiro let us go home. My nightmare was over, and my son was happy and in less pain and so much straighter. It was amazing what Dr. Shapiro had accomplished. I asked Kyle, "Aren't you happy that we did this surgery, that I didn't let you go through a painful death?" Kyle smiled, and I gave him a kiss and told him, "Together we will get through anything. Let's go home and see your sisters!

Months passed. Kyle was doing great and was adjusting to not wearing his body jacket. His muscle tone was still very high, making him lean to the right side. I thought that maybe we should have kept him in the body jacket, but now he was used to not having one on. Kyle wanted no part of wearing one ever again. His muscle tone had curved his feet, rotated his hip out of socket, re-curved his right foot again, and taken his spine. I wondered where the muscle tone would go next?

Well, it didn't take long to find out. The tension went to his neck. Losing movement and forming a left-side neglect made it hard for him to drive his motorized wheelchair. Children's Hospital Nopco Department a man named Rusty came up with a solution by making an extension to Kyle's headrest near his forehead. This would help to keep his head up and would fight against his muscle tone going to the right side. It was a challenge we had every day. We were still increasing his Baclofen pump every month.

Kyle and I decided to try Botox in his neck, shoulders, left arm, fingers, and legs. Botox is a muscle injection that relaxes the muscles, and we had been having good results. Dr. Donna Nimec performs this procedure every ten to twelve weeks with a mild sedation at Children Hospital. The only bad thing is that it is temporary it last about eight to ten weeks and involves many needles.

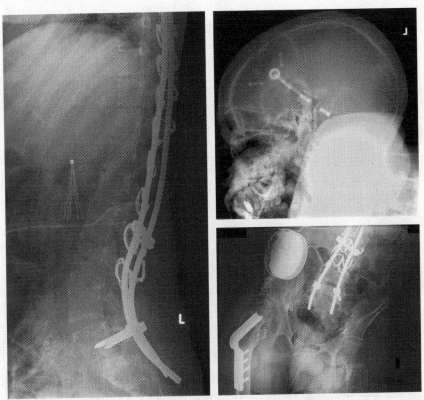

Kyle's X-Rays displaying the hardware within his body:
1) Posterior Spinal fusion, two rods the size of a pinky finger
wrapped with wire from pelvis to below the neck.
2) VP shunt
3) Baclofen Pump with a catheter connected to spinal cord, and
a dislocated hip held in place by a plate and screws.

Chapter 30

It was a gorgeous day outside. Birds were singing, flowers were blooming, and I thought it was a great day to take Kyle and the girls for a walk. This was one of the kids' favorite things to do, because we made it a mystery walk. Today it was Kim's turn, and we started at Wells Junior High School.

I said, "Take me to the Rez (the old swimming area)." Kim had no idea where to go, but she started off. The rest of us didn't say anything, even though she was going in the wrong direction, and we walked for over an hour. Kim finally gave up and asked Kyle for help. Kyle smiled, feeling proud that he could help her, and drove his motorized wheelchair in the direction of the Rez. When we arrived at the bottom of the street, Kim started to giggle. "Now I know where I am," she said, and she led us the rest of the way. The mystery walk was a fun activity, and I loved the fact that Kyle hadn't lost any memory about his hometown. I was always amazed at how smart he was. I also loved it that Kyle could still teach his sisters. It made him feel so proud.

Kyle was due for another surgery, and this one was easy. It was a replacement of the battery in his Baclofen pump, something we had to do every six or seven years. It was a three- to four-hour surgery that required a two- to three-day hospital stay. Having been through so many surgeries, we called this one a piece of cake. Kyle had no fear, saying, "I'm just going for a nap and to see the gorgeous nurses." Kyle was always a flirt with a great sense of humor, and we made the best of our visit.

A few months went by, and Kyle had a low-grade fever. His temperature never went up unless something was seriously wrong. I tried to break the fever, but nothing worked. I took him to Children's Hospital once again. Since Kyle seemed fine and had no other symptoms, he thought it was a joke. He knew his body didn't show symptoms and that he was always a puzzle to the doctors.

In the emergency room, the staff checked him out. His fever was up to 102 degrees. Kyle smiled and flirted, acting like nothing was wrong. The doctor asked, "Does anything hurt?" Kyle laughed and said, "My balls." Embarrassed, I said, "Kyle!" But that's my boy. The doctor smiled and said, "Well, besides that." With a smile, Kyle said no. Everything looked great on Kyle, but we waited for the blood test results. His levels were a little elevated, and the doctor said we had to wait twenty-four to forty-eight hours to see if anything would grow in his blood culture. To be on the safe side, the doctor decided to admit Kyle, as his fever still would not break.

The next day came, and Kyle was still laughing and telling jokes. Thank God, no one could understand his speech except me. He was hard to understand because he didn't have a lot of airflow or strength to be loud, especially in his chair. When he was in bed, a person could actually hold a conversation with him and understand what he was saying. Kyle and I were reading some cards that my sister Gina had made him. They were hilarious. Dr. Madsen came in and asked what we were laughing about. I told him that my sister always made cards for Kyle to make him laugh. Then I quickly changed the subject, as I didn't want the doctor to read them. I would have been embarrassed.

I asked Dr. Madsen if the blood test had come back. He said, "Yes. Kyle has a staph infection, which is very serious. It's targeting all the hardware in his body. He has a shunt, a Baclofen pump, two rods wrapped with wire around his spine, metal in his hip and foot, and a filter screen. We are not really sure, but we are guessing that the infection is in the shunt and Baclofen pump."

I thought, *Okay, we'll give him some strong antibiotics and then, hopefully, the infection will go away.* But the doctor said, "We can't heal an infection around steel or a shunt. The inside, where the fluid flows, has to be replaced." That was when I realized that we were again facing major surgery. Kyle was listening, and there was no more laughter or smiling or telling jokes. He just looked confused.

Dr. Madsen explained that this was life threatening. The infection was very serious, and Kyle needed surgery the next morning. His shunt would be removed and replaced by a temporary one. His pump would be removed as well, but it couldn't be replaced until that part of his spine healed, and that could take up to six months.

Six months! What about Kyle's spasms? He would be in so much pain; he wouldn't be able to handle it. I began tearing up, shocked at what I was being told. How could this be? There had been no other symptoms—no headaches, no loss of appetite, no vomiting, nothing. The doctor looked puzzled also. He said that normally a person with this infection would be deathly sick, but Kyle's only symptom was a fever. Still, we knew that Kyle's body never showed symptoms until we were far into the problem. In cases like this, it just wasn't good.

I called home, crying, and shared the news with my family. I was as scared as I could be. Alone with Kyle, I thought about what was ahead—especially the spasms. His spasms being so bad, they curved his whole body. How would we get through this? I told my girls that I had to stay in the hospital with Kyle. I tried to explain about Kyle's infection and his need for surgery, which was a lot for them to handle. I always felt that I should be honest and tell them the truth, because I never knew what would happen with Kyle from one day to the next. The girls needed to understand that when Kyle was in a lot of pain, I couldn't be home with them. They were in tears, saying that they wanted to be with Kyle. I told them that Kyle would be in surgery the next day and would be sleeping. I said they could visit him in a few days, and they were good with that. I said I would talk to them tomorrow.

Morning came, and I told Kyle everything was going to be okay. He had his stuffed bear and Daddy's picture with him. Kyle knew he was having surgery, but he didn't realize the extent of it, and he started telling his jokes. This time, because he was lying down, his voice was loud, and the nurses and doctors could understand him. I was so embarrassed. I apologized, but I was also laughing. I said, "Whatever we need to do to make him happy." They agreed. Off Kyle went, laughing away and putting on his lemonade mask for good luck, to fall asleep.

I returned to the waiting room once again, never having thought I would be there so soon again. We had only come in because of a fever—not for a surgery! I waited by myself, as Lenny was at work. The waiting was long and hard, but I preferred to do it alone. All the hospital stays and surgeries were starting to affect our relationship. I called my sister Patty and cried with her. Then I called another family member to give updates, trying to stay positive. I did a lot of praying and talking to Mike, as that always seemed to comfort me. I felt that Mike was with me all the time. Although I was alone, my heart was filled with Mike. I knew that God was watching over Kyle, and I prayed for strength to overcome this battle also.

Surgery took all day, and Kyle came through it well. He had a temporary shunt in his head for drainage of fluid but no Baclofen Pump to help with his spasms. Kyle was on heavy medication and antibiotics, and I knew that we had a long road to go down. Dr. Madsen said we weren't out of the woods yet and wouldn't know how Kyle was until we saw that the antibiotics were working and the fever was gone.

Days went by, and they felt very long. Kyle was alert, in pain, and having spasms. The medicine was not working, and they gave him Valium, as needed, with morphine. Kyle was sweating, and I put cold towels on his forehead, thinking back to when we had come home from Spaulding. Kyle had to lie on his back and could only have his bed at a little tilt. The temporary shunt was draining so much fluid; I was shocked to see what came out of him. The girls called, wanting to come down, but Kyle was not good, so I had to hold them off a little. I missed them so much, but I didn't want them to see their brother in all this pain. It was hard enough for me to handle, never mind their young ages.

Dr. Madsen kept telling me to prepare myself for anything to happen. We wouldn't know Kyle's condition until we saw the results in his blood. I couldn't even think about the end possibilities, but I realized that such things did happen. My neighbor in the next room was watching her son die. Seeing that family suffer was just horrible. I cried for them and couldn't imagine losing my little boy. Their son died later that day.

After a week, I had Lenny and the girls come to visit. It was so nice to see my family. They stayed the whole day with us, and Kyle was so happy. Overall, he had a good day, and the spasms were not as bad. I asked the doctor how long he thought we would be in the hospital. He said it might be two more weeks, depending on the blood test. I looked at Kyle and thought, *two more weeks to go!*

Each day I waited for news of his blood test. "Some results are in," said Dr. Madsen. "The blood is not growing anything. So far so good." This meant that the antibiotics were working. I asked what the next step was. He said that they would go back in and put in another shunt in a couple of days, but they couldn't put the Baclofen pump back for six months. I didn't like that, as Kyle was still having spasms. It was going to be a hard and long six months.

I was excited when company came to visit. Over the span of two days, my parents, Uncle Ronald, Aunt Gloria, and Meme Rita came down. It was so nice. Their visits broke up the days and made them go by much faster. I was thinking positive thoughts. Nearly two weeks had passed, and Kyle was going back into surgery. He just wanted to be able to sit up again and to be able to sleep on his side.

Surgery took a few hours and was a success. Kyle came back to his room, all bundled up and looking exhausted. I thought about how much this little body had endured in the last seven years. After eighteen surgeries, he was a miracle, and I thought how lost I would be without him.

I slept on a chair that turned into a foldout bed every night, and it was so uncomfortable, it was like sleeping on springs. Kyle and I made jokes, laughed, and were silly, just to make the time go by faster. I would have given anything to have a real bed, especially because of my back and arm injuries. After a week, I got smart and had Lenny bring me an egg-crate pad, and it definitely helped. One night I had to share my little bed with Katie, as she was having a hard time being away from Kyle and me. Just watching her sleep, I thought of everything my poor little girls had been through. Their lives had been flipped upside down. All I could do was to be there as much as I could and to let them know how much their daddy and I loved them.

Another week went by—with no more fevers. Kyle was doing great, and we could go home. Oh, did that sound good! Kyle was still in pain with spasms, but at least we knew the infection wasn't getting worse and we were out of danger. Kyle came home on twenty-eight pills a day. I was a pharmacy!

It was a very long five months of pain, and I called Dr Madsen, asking him to put the pump in early. The doctor agreed, as Kyle just couldn't take it any longer. His spirits were low, and eating was difficult. I felt that we were losing everything we had worked for because of his spasms. This was one surgery we couldn't get past fast enough.

Kyle and I were so happy to arrive at the hospital. We were excited for him to be taken to the operating room, asking for a lemonade mask, to fall fast asleep while holding his little bear tightly. The surgery took a few hours. I was excited to see my little boy wake up soon after he heard my voice. I was relieved that the surgery was done. I am so thankful to Dr. Madson for his knowledge and experience with the shunt and baclofen pump. Kyle would of never survived without them. Dr. Berde did some bolus feeds of Baclofen to get the medicine into his system faster. Kyle did well, and we went back every week to adjust the medicine.

In no time, he was back to the old Kyle. He could tolerate the little spasms, and he smiled and joked, excited to go back to school. I was fortunate that Kyle was so good-natured. He knew that he was loved, and he was a busy little guy. Even when things went wrong medically, he always kept that great smile on his face, and his gorgeous blue eyes always sparkled.

Chapter 31

Kyle was seventeen and a handsome young man. His smile was so innocent, his blue eyes so bright, and he had a personality and sense of humor that would bring a smile to anyone's face. This would have been his senior year of high school in his hometown of Southbridge, Massachusetts. He knew all his classmates would be graduating soon, and he thought about everything he had missed in the last seven years, wishing he could be with his friends.

At times, he ran into them. Some were shy or scared, not knowing what to say to their classmate. They felt sad for him, seeing his twisted body sitting paralyzed in a wheelchair. He had trouble speaking, and they could only imagine what he had gone through. Kyle's eyes would light up like a Christmas tree if a girl classmate would just hold his hand and talk to him. If he was lucky, she might give him a kiss on the cheek. It made Kyle so happy if a boy classmate talked to him about the sports they used to play together, what was happening in their life, and what trouble they were getting into. All Kyle wanted was a little attention.

Watching these reunions always brought me to tears, making me think about what could have been but never would be. I also realized how lucky I was to still have my son—and how proud I was of him. Seeing Kyle's friends also made me miss them even more. I had missed seeing them all grow into young adults, missed the times they would have been over at our house, sharing fun times and raiding the refrigerator. Kyle and I had missed out on a lot, but we treasured what we did have and the times we got to see everyone.

We ran into a classmate at a game, and she invited Kyle to go to their senior prom. Kyle had been so excited. His cousin Holly was a junior at the time, and she offered to go with him. Holly, looking beautiful in her beige, long sparkling gown. Kyle looked very handsome in a black tuxedo. He was excited to be with his friends and was feeling like one of the guys. But he was so excited that he became very tense. His muscles were very tight, and he started to sweat. He was also wishing he could feed himself or just stand up to have a special dance with his own special girl. In reality, he knew it couldn't happen, but he was okay with that. At least he was with his peers. He didn't want the night to end.

Holly was a great cousin to help fulfill her cousin's dream of attending his senior prom. She had a busy night, helping Kyle with all his needs and giving him a great time. His friends said good-bye, hoping he would participate in graduation with them. Kyle put his thumbs up to let them know he would. He couldn't wait until the next time he would see them all again.

We needed to get permission for Kyle to participate in the graduation, and the school committee said yes. On graduation day, Kyle marched down with his classmates, being pushed in his wheelchair by one of his friends, feeling so proud in his red cap and gown. Graduation was nice. We listened to the choir and the speeches and watched his classmates receive scholarships. I sat in the bleachers with a big smile and tears in my eyes, admiring my handsome son. I was so happy for him that he could share this day with his classmates.

I watched Kyle's sisters, Kimberly and Katie; go to the podium to present a scholarship to their brother in memory of their father, Michael Brodeur. Katie spoke about their father, describing how he had been taken at the young age of thirty-nine by a drunk driver. She said that he would have been proud of Kyle and so proud of all his accomplishments. No matter how many surgeries and obstacles Kyle had gone through, he'd always had a smile. She said that he was their hero and inspiration, and they were thankful to have him in their lives, inspiring them to go after their goals. They told him that he was the best brother in the world and that they loved him.

Walking over to Kyle, they handed him the scholarship, and each of them gave Kyle a kiss. The audience clapped loudly and gave him a standing ovation. I was speechless, overwhelmed, and so proud of all three of my children. I wished that Mike were there with me, holding my hand. After graduation, Kyle took pictures with his friends, and many people congratulated him. It was so nice, and I was so thankful that Kyle could be part of it. The next day, we had a huge party at our house filled with red and white balloons and decorations. One hundred and fifty people came throughout the day. Kyle had a day filled with excitement, and he felt loved. He will always remember it.

A few months later, we were back in the hospital. Kyle was sweating and having severe spasms. Dr. Berde checked his Baclofen pump and it read that it was okay. I said the pump wasn't working, even though the pump showed that it was. After two days of trying to figure out what was happening, Kyle was in severe withdrawal. I asked the doctor to go in and see if there was medicine in the pump. Even though the pump showed that there was medicine, it didn't make sense that he was having withdrawal symptoms.

Since there was no other explanation for Kyle's withdrawal, Dr. Berde agreed. To his amazement, the pump was empty. It had malfunctioned. The team of doctors was shocked. Where had the medicine gone? No one knew. This meant that Kyle had to have surgery to put a new battery in. At that point, Kyle was suffering so badly that he just wanted to be in a deep sleep. Surgery was scheduled to take place as soon as possible. Dr. Madsen put in a new battery and checked to make sure the catheter was still in place on his spinal cord. Dr. Berde filled Kyle's pump with medicine and administered a few bolus feeds to get it into his system fast. Kyle spasms were manageable once again. What a relief! One thing I loved about Dr. Berde was that he always listened to my opinion, and always said, "A mother knows her child best". I felt so blessed to have him for Kyle.

Life at home was busy, and the girls were in cheering competitions every weekend. During the week, they practiced, did homework, and visited Kyle at school. I was always dealing with insurance issues and doctors' appointments. The weekends went by so fast, and I always tried to get in a walk with Kyle or to play games or do anything he wanted to do. His sisters, Cassie and Breanna, came over a lot, and we never had a chance to get bored. Our lives were filled with so much love, and we were blessed to have such a big family.

Lenny felt like I was Mike's wife, not his. He was tired of all the courts dates, media, and newspapers. We have been to court numerous times over the years with appeals; it seemed to fill our house with some anxiety, as we didn't know what would happen. It was a lot for him to handle, especially with my arm injuries and the days when I was bedridden or couldn't walk. All the time spent away at hospitals and going through surgeries was taking a toll on our relationship. Lenny worked six days a week, and we didn't have much time together. It was very difficult, but I knew there wasn't much I could do about it. My life was hard, and I had to be there for my kids.

I was determined to be the best mother I could be and to bring up my kids to be happy. I prayed to Mike and God to give me the strength I needed to get through every day. It was difficult raising my children without their father, and I always reminded my kids that Daddy was there with us, just in a different way. I told them that he was watching over us, so they'd better be good!

Chapter 32

It had been about six years since a drunk driver had shattered our lives. We had been down a rocky road, but as a family, we'd fought to stay strong and overcome all our obstacles. We had learned so much that we decided we wanted to start doing drunk-driving presentations at schools. A few years back, a teacher at the Dudley Middle School, Mrs. Claudette Eagleton, had approached me but I just hadn't been ready at the time. She had called me again a year later, and our conversation made me think that it was time—and might help us with the healing process. I thought that if we could reach at least one student, it would be worth the time and effort we put into making a presentation.

I didn't know where to start. When the kids came home from school, I asked them what they thought about doing presentations. Kyle gave a thumbs-up and a big smile, and Kim and Katie thought it was a great idea. As a family, we worked hard for a few weeks, putting together a video presentation.

We started the video with Mike's CD playing in the background and family pictures of the way we had been before the accident. Next, we showed the demolished vehicles and talked about what had happened in the crash. There were pictures of Kyle in a coma, on a ventilator, with a feeding tube in his nose, attached to a heart monitor, and so on. More pictures showed Kyle coming out of his coma months later—and how thin he was as he sat in a wheelchair. We added a video of physical therapy and Kyle's piercing cries when he was not happy on a big ball.

We showed how we'd taken care of Kyle—using lifts, transporting him, giving him a bath, and getting him dressed. We explain all eighteen of his surgeries and showed us putting him in a body jacket, the brace that covered his torso.

Kimberly and Katie each read about what had happened to them in the accident. They described their fears and missing their daddy. They said that they would give anything to be able to sit on his lap one more time. They told about how hard it was for them to watch their friends with their daddies, knowing that they would never have their own father again. They said that they had watched their brother suffer in pain all the time, that their mom had stayed with Kyle at the hospitals, and that they had always been worried that their brother wouldn't come back home. They talked about how much Kyle missed his friends and wished they were around. Life was different.

Next, we played the "Hero" song alongside pictures that showed Kyle's progress from his coma to where he was today. We showed how much he had fought to be where he was and that he had never given up. The cemetery photos showed were Mike was buried and how we sent balloons off to him with special messages on special occasions and visits. At the end, Kyle spoke a special message: "Please don't drink and drive."

After the video presentation, we put students in a wheelchair, a body jacket, and a full body cast and asked how they felt. They didn't like it. It was very uncomfortable, and they couldn't wait to get out of it. Kids asked us questions, many of them in tears. They were shocked to see what happened in an accident like this. I was in tears myself, and answering questions was difficult. It felt good when the presentation was over. I felt like I had reached the kids, and they learned something from this.

A few weeks later, we received letters from the kids, and my children and I read them. Some of them had me in tears, as they said they had received the message to not drink and drive and not to do drugs. Some had wounds opened in their own lives, having a parent who drank a lot, and they asked us how to stop that parent from getting behind a wheel before they hurt someone or themselves. The student having the fear of living a life like Kyle and realizing that handicap people are just like them. Special needs people just want to be loved and accepted like everyone else.

We did several presentations for a couple of years in grade eight through twelve. I even had a student come to me after receiving a driver's license to tell me that he would never forget what I'd taught them—to never drink and drive or do drugs. I felt good about that. I thought, *this could be the one student who remembers and whose life I might have changed!*

Months later, I receive a phone call from Keith's probation officer, Geraldo Alicea. He told me that Keith had been arrested after obtaining a license illegally, speeding, and driving on the wrong side of the road. He had tested positive for cocaine use, and he hadn't been doing his community service. I sat down and asked, "What does this all mean? Did he hurt someone else?" Mr. Alicea said no that no one else had been involved, and I replied, "Thank God." He said we would have to go back to court for a hearing because Keith had gone against his probation, and he would most likely end up back in prison if he was found guilty.

I was relieved that no one had been hurt. I had always known that it was only a matter of time before I would get a phone call like this. I knew that this man just didn't care, and I wanted him back in jail. I felt that he'd only gotten a slap on the wrist the first time, and this time he should get the maximum sentence.

I waited anxiously for the kids to come home from school, and then I shared with them what Keith had done. The girls asked if he had hurt someone. I said no, and they were relieved. I told the kids that this meant we would be going back to court eventually, and I asked them if they would be willing to write victim statements. Katie and Kimberly looked at each other and said yes. Then they asked, "What do we write?"

I told them to write whatever came to their minds. I said that there was no right or wrong, that they could tell the judge and Keith about their feelings and talk about Daddy, their brother, and what they were missing. Off they went to their rooms for a couple of hours. I wrote a few pages myself. Once I started writing, I found I had so much to say.

When they came downstairs, the girls took turns reading what they'd written. Kimberly was thirteen and Katie was eleven, and as I listened to them, I was amazed at how grown-up they were. I understood that they had missed out on being with their father, but I also realized that they had made the best out of a horrible situation. I hugged them both with pride, feeling blessed that these two young ladies were mine.

Friday came, and Kyle's bus pulled into the driveway. The girls ran to the bus to help him get off, grabbing his bags and giving him kisses, having so much to tell him. Kyle came into the house with the girls pushing his wheelchair. They said, "Mom! Tell Kyle about Keith!" Kyle's eyes were big, and he looked right at me very seriously.

I said, "Keith went against his probation by obtaining a license, speeding, and driving on the wrong side of the road. He tested positive for cocaine and was not doing his community service. That means he could go back to prison if he is found guilty. Kyle smiled and gave thumbs up. I asked him if he would like to write a letter to the judge and Keith, telling them what Keith took from him and what he was feeling. Kyle put on a big smile again and spelled on his alphabet board, "I have lots to tell him."

I said, "Okay. When you feel like working on it, we will do it together, and your sisters will help too." He wanted to start right away, and off he went with his sisters. It took a few weeks to get Kyle's letter done, as he had so much to say. I was so proud of him. He really put a lot of thought into it, and it brought me to tears, hearing my son's thoughts about what had been taken from him.

The day arrived for us to go to court again. This time my children were older, and they understood more about what was going to happen. They knew they would see Keith, the man who had killed their father. My girls were excited to see what would happen in court, and they acted very grown-up. They weren't nervous about going on the witness stand. They had so much they wanted to tell Keith and the judge about how their lives had changed. The TV stations were present, and the newspapers were interviewing us. The children were very mature about the whole thing. They'd had a lot of experience with the media all these years. Doing presentations and being in hospitals had made them grow up quickly for their ages.

Keith came into the courtroom. Kyle was now nineteen. He was aware and out of his coma, and he really wanted to take a good look at Keith. Kimberly and Katie wanted to understand why he didn't have any feelings or show any emotion. "Doesn't he care that he took our daddy away from us?" Kimberly asked. I just gave her a hug, as the judge was coming in and we had to be quiet.

Judge John McCann was the affiliating judge. Judge Daniel F. Toomey, who sentenced Keith the first time, had passed away. Judge McCann had reviewed the case and stated that Keith had several parole violations. He listed each one aloud, stating that Keith had obtained a motor vehicle license, had failed to surrender his license, had been speeding and driving on the wrong side of the road, had tested positive to cocaine, and had not been doing his community service. Before sentencing Keith, the judge allowed my family to get up and speak, one at a time.

Kimberly went first. She looked Keith right in the eye and told him how hard it was for her and her sister to watch their brother in so much pain all the time. They felt so helpless. It just wasn't fair that he'd had so many losses—and eighteen surgeries. Losing their father had been especially hard on Kyle because he was the oldest. Being so injured, Kyle couldn't show emotion or even cry. His speech was very difficult to understand, so he spelled things out on his alphabet board. Kyle couldn't do anything for himself. He was in diapers, and he had no privacy at all. He was frustrated and angry at times, because he missed his old life—the sports, the friends, and his independence—and he wanted a girlfriend so badly.

Kimberly went on. "Those times when Kyle and my mom are in hospitals for weeks at a time, it's hard on my sister and me. Sometimes we call her, and Kyle is in so much pain that my mom is crying because she can't take his pain away. We worry that Kyle won't get better, and we wonder if someday he won't come home. When the pain is so bad for him, he says he wishes he could just die. Then we have to try to make him happy and help him focus on the good in his life."

Looking at Judge McCann, Kimberly said, "If you could spend one day with our family and see how Kyle suffers and what we do as a family, you would understand why it's important to us that Keith isn't able to drive ever again—and why he should go back to prison. Keith has had many chances, and he has failed over and over again. My brother will never get a second chance, and we will never see my father again. Keith is a danger to our society. Please get him off our roads." She thanked the judge, looked at Keith again, and then walked past him to her seat.

Katie walked up and stood at the podium. She told Judge McCann and Keith that she and her sister would never know their father, as they had only been three and five years old at the time of the accident. They only knew him through videos and pictures and what people told them. She said it was hard to visit their friends who had dads. She and her sister wished they had a dad, so they could sit on his lap and get hugs and kisses from him. They would never know what that felt like. Entering the teenage years would be hard without his guidance. Their father wouldn't be there for graduation or college. He wouldn't be at their weddings to give them away. He would never see their children. Keith had taken so much away from them.

Katie continued. "On Father's Day and my dad's birthday, we celebrate by going to the cemetery with balloons. We write special messages to him and attach them to the balloons, hoping he will receive them. All we can do is pray and talk to him for our comfort. Someday, Keith, you will lose your dad, and you will go visit him at a cemetery. Then you will realize what you have taken from us. But we were much younger than you. At least you got to know your dad. You took our chance away, because you chose to drink, drive, and do drugs. Your honor, please consider the longest prison term possible. Our family still suffers every day. Keith has received many chances, but he doesn't care about the court system or how it works. He makes his own rules. Please don't let him hurt another family like he did ours. I wouldn't wish this on anyone." Katie thanked the judge and walked past Keith. Keith looked down.

Then it was my turn. I was shaking and angry as I looked at him, thinking of how he had taken my husband and ruined my son's life. I wished I still had my husband, but I couldn't change what had happened. I looked at the judge and stated that the last eight years had been terribly difficult for my children and me. I went over Kyle's eighteen surgeries—some of which had been ten to twelve hours long— and described his severe muscle tone and constant pain. I told the court that we had spent over a year in a hospital. Keith could do everything he wanted—get married, have children, walk, feed himself, and enjoy all the simple pleasures in life. Kyle couldn't. His body wouldn't allow him to. And Mike was in a casket. He had lost all the enjoyments of life at only thirty-nine years of age. Kyle was a prisoner in his own body, with no second chance to change anything.

I said that Keith had been given several chances and had failed. He couldn't even follow his probation rules. He didn't want to grow up. He just made his own rules. Keith had committed manslaughter and had disabled me. He had permanently disabled my son for life. I said that Keith should go back to prison for killing my husband. There he could obtain the help he needed, and hopefully he would never be able to obtain a driver's license again. I thanked the judge and asked if Kyle could join me, because he had written a statement also. Keith's attorney did not want Kyle to go up, but the judge allowed it.

With Kyle at my side, I read his statement to Keith. "Eight years ago, all I asked from you was not to drink, drive, or do drugs. But being the irresponsible person that you are, you did. You took everything from me—all the sports, my teenage years, proms, girls, having children, and making my mom a grandmother. You even took away the best father I could have had, and I think of him every day.

"At the age of eleven, I had to go to school, a special school away from home, like a college. I was petrified and in so much pain that I had to trust doctors and nurses to care for me. My mom and sisters traveled to Canton to be with me all the time so I could feel loved and safe. It was very hard for me to adjust. It took a long time.

"I had so many surgeries. You should try having a body cast for three long months, sweating and itching and having no way to scratch. I have so much hardware in my body that I always have to worry about infection. I have rods, shunts, plates, screws, a Baclofen pump, and a filter screen. That is a lot of hardware for one person.

"Keith, you could never walk in my shoes, even if you tried. You are too weak. You don't have the strength or courage that I have, or we wouldn't be here today. I have to go through all this torture of pain and suffering. I can't understand why you won't obey the laws of the court. I would give anything to be free from my body, but I don't have the privilege of getting that chance. You get many chances and still fail."

Kyle's letter then addressed the judge. "Your Honor, this man took my father's life and my life also. Would you please let him serve the rest of his probation time in prison, since I am in prison for the rest of my life?"

I thanked the judge, and Kyle and I went back to our seats. Kyle gave Keith his middle finger.

Norman, Michael's brother and a Southbridge police officer, approached the front of the room and said to the judge, "Keith is laughing at this court. Judge McCann, he slapped you and me in the face by getting a license. He deserves a long jail sentence. He has received forty-seven individual citations in the past sixteen years and his license has been suspended numerous times. I was on duty the night of the accident, and I saw my brother dead in the front seat and my nieces lying in the roadway. I wondered how I was going to tell my mother that her son had just been killed. This man has served only three years for killing my brother, putting my nephew in a wheelchair for the rest of his life, and breaking up a family. He belongs in jail for a long time." Norman thanked the judge and asked him to do the right thing to keep our roads safe.

Before sentencing Keith, Judge McCann said, "In my eleven and a half years as a judge, I have never seen such flagrant disregard for conditions of parole." Then he sentenced Keith to serve nine to twelve years in prison for six parole violations.

Holding my children's hands and hearing the sentence, I cried. Finally, some justice would be served! My children were in tears also, and Kyle was wearing a big smile. We'd done it! The roads would be safe, at least from him, for nine more years. I looked up and said, "Mike, there is finally some justice for you. I love you!"

Another court day was past, but through the years we have been to court many more times, especially with appeals. It seems never-ending. I'd thought we were done after this last hearing, but things were far from over. A request for reconsideration of Keith's state prison sentence, made in a court motion, alleged corruption among public officials, because he had obtained a drivers license with the aid of public officials. Judge John S. McCann dismissed this motion on procedural grounds without a hearing. So Keith's attorney filed a appeal, and Keith's allegations became the subject of a Suffolk County grand jury investigation.

Keith had paid Lawrence Trapasso—a city election commissioner and former employee of the state auditor's office—to get a driver's license and restore his right to drive, even though a judge had ordered his license suspended for seven years. Mr. Trapasso had promised to clear Keith's driving record through bribery. In 2005 Keith had paid Mr. Trapasso five thousand dollars to fix his license problem. Ten days later, Mr. Trapasso allegedly asked for another six thousand dollars because the victims in the case were "pushing probation." However, he assured Keith that the probation condition prohibiting the convicted felon from driving for seven years would be removed.

Mr. Trapasso had called Keith and told him the condition was removed and that Keith could go to the Worcester RMV office and get his license. He obtained his learner's permit at the Worcester RMV. Later that month, Mr. Trapasso told Keith to go to the Chinatown RMV office and take the driver's test. After doing so, he had gotten his driver's license. Keith had also paid $1,250 for tickets to a charity dinner to meet various public officials, but Mr. Trapasso had kept the money without bringing Keith to the dinner.

Keith's attorney filed a motion seeking reconsideration of his lengthy prison sentence on the basis of ineffective legal representation and a failure to take into account certain mental problems that Keith had suffered at the time. These problems had pushed him to make bad decisions that were influenced by "corrupt officials who took advantage of him." Keith's appeal was denied, and he would serve his sentence of at least nine years.

It amazed me to learn what Keith had done to get around the judicial system. I was so thankful that he had been caught—and that Mr. Trapasso was also found guilty. Mr. Trapasso was sentenced to two to three years in state prison for larceny of property worth over $250 and three counts of public corruption. Mr. Trapasso was convicted of offering to help three people, including Mr. Doucette, to get their suspended driver's licenses back or to avoid losing them.

It's been almost seven years now, and Keith will come up for parole in a couple of years. We will go back to court again before a panel of three judges in Boston, and they will decide when Keith will get out. This time, though, when he gets out, he will be a free man—no probation or restrictions. I just hope he has learned something during all these years in prison and realizes that drugs and alcohol are not the answer. I hope to God that he never gets behind a wheel ever again. That will be up to the Registry of Motor Vehicles to decide. It's not about the Brodeur family any longer. It's about keeping all of society safe.

Chapter 33

Kyle is twenty-one years old now. He has loved his school program and realizes that the school he has been attending for eleven years will be coming to an end. Lots of exciting things are going on. He has been working on a speech device that he is finally willing to learn. For the last three years, he hadn't been interested in using one. Kyle will finally have a voice! He will also use pictures and spell out sentences to tell us what his needs and wants are. The speech device will help people to understand him better, and he will be able to communicate with us much faster. His therapist had been trying for years to find one that was compatible with Kyle, but he hadn't been interested until this year. It was a huge step forward.

We are trying to transition Kyle from his school program to his new day program, which begins when he turns twenty-two. Visiting the day program at the Center of Hope was a big change from his school. Kyle will have his own one-to-one help every day, with his own vehicle to take him wherever he would like to go. The people at the Center of Hope are very nice and are willing to help with the transition in any way they can. Kyle was also fitted for a new motorized wheelchair, and he must make the big decision about what color it will be. With so much happening, the year has just flown by.

Mass Hospital School had their junior prom, with the girls in gorgeous gowns and the guys in tuxedos. Kyle attended with a beautiful girl from his hometown. The students and their dates were all transported by a special handicap bus to a great restaurant with a big room to dance in. Pictures were taken as they arrived, and a sit-down hot meal was prepared for them. There were lots of tables with decorations on them but few chairs, because most people were in wheelchairs. With a DJ and gorgeous decorations, it was a night the kids would never forget. Staff from the school attended with the kids, and they danced and had a great time. Of course, they also crowned a king and queen. They had so much fun; they didn't want the night to end. What a night! It was a demonstration of the love and dedication the school provided each and every day, and it showed in the students' smiles. It was a wonderful prom, and everyone was very happy.

Then the "big day" arrived, the one Kyle had heard about when he first started the school at eleven years of age. He was going to Walt Disney World for a class trip with his senior classmates! Dick Crisafolli dedicates so much time and effort to put this magical trip together for all the seniors. This trip took a year just to plan. Ten students would be graduating, and the trip was paid for by the school's fundraising efforts. Each student would take both of his or her wheelchairs, in case one broke down. Any students who were not in wheelchairs would bring along any equipment they might need. Hospital beds were delivered to the resort for each student, along with a bed for the one-to-ones. There was a nurse for all medication, a doctor for any emergencies, and special straps and wedges needed for bedtime and rides for each student. All clothing, diapers, special medical supplies, braces, and so on were provided for each child's needs. They all received huge, blue tote bags with "Mass Hospital School" on them and jackets with the students' names on them. The students were excited to go, and all of them had huge smiles from ear to ear, knowing that this was going to be so much fun. Some students were going to Walt Disney World for the first time, and this was a dream-come-true for all of them.

The week went by so fast. Kyle came home with so much to say, smiling from ear to ear with his thumbs up. He'd had a great time with all his friends. He told me he had gone on the Rocking Roller Coaster ride, the Tower of Terror, and every ride he could do. I said, "You're nuts!" I felt sick to my stomach, knowing that he'd gone on those dangerous rides. I wondered how he had even done it, being paralyzed and having no upper body control. I was told that Kyle had been able to go on those rides because he was held in place with straps. I still thought there was no way, and I didn't want to think about it. I was so glad I wasn't there to witness it. He had definitely taken a trip that he would never forget. He even received a DVD they'd made of their special trip, with Disney music and a beautiful album full of pictures. I felt so happy that my son had enjoyed such a great class trip!

I thought back about Kyle's first days at MHS. They had been so scary for me. Kyle had been in his coma, and I'd been so afraid to leave my little boy. He had only been eleven years old. Kyle being a real mystery in the beginning, trying to figure out what he remembered. Could he read and comprehend and retain what was being taught to him? What would be the best way to teach him and keep his attention? Kyle being on so much medicine was a challenge to keep him alert. Using cold towels and keeping him out of discomfort with his spasms and severe muscle tone was a full time job in itself. His teacher Marion Peck and aid Kathy Carroll figured it all out in time and as the years went by Kyle did wonderful in school. As Kyle had gotten older and we had adjusted more, we'd had some good and bad months. Medically, Kyle had always been a challenge. With so many surgeries and recoveries, it felt, at times, like he was home more often than he was at school. He would be doing great, and then a surgery would need to be done, followed by another setback and the need to start over. Wheelchair adjustments had to be made often. Thanks to Gary Rabideau and Cathy Ellis, they are amazing at what they do. They work miracles for so many students.

With his great personality and sense of humor, Kyle had always loved the staff and students. Sometimes he would clash with a staff member, it would make things hard, but we worked it out and got through it. Every few years, we went through changes with doctors, case management, teachers, one-to-ones, therapists, and cottages. Those changes were always a big adjustment for Kyle and me. Sometimes they were good changes, and other times they weren't.

Every year Kyle went through a month of depression that started in October. The anniversary of our accident was November 1st, and his depression always lasted until the middle or end of November. Kyle would act out and get in a lot of trouble at school. I dreaded this time of year, as I always received a lot of phone calls about Kyle's behavior. It was very hard on him. I had a difficult time also, with a week or two when I cried very easily. I tried to stay strong and positive and reminded Kyle to focus on what we did have. Kyle always missed his old life, when he'd been able to walk and do everything for himself. It was always a very hard month, and missing his father made it even worse for him.

Kyle wasn't always a angel at school, and I received phone calls about his behavior all the time. Some reports said that he touched others inappropriately, rammed into others' wheelchairs, folded kids up in bed, or broke people's DVDs by throwing them on the floor and running over them with his chair. He even pulled a fire alarm by an elevator, and the school had to be evacuated. There was always something. I got to the point that I didn't want to answer my phone at night. What was I supposed to say? Okay, Kyle had been put to bed early again or had lost his recreation night. Those weeks I just wanted Friday to come so I could have my son home.

I'd always felt like I'd sent my child to college at the age of eleven. It felt like a college. It had a lake, a pontoon boat, a barn full of horses, goats, and other animals, a racetrack, a bowling alley, a indoor swimming pool, a huge gym for playing every sport with wheelchairs, a radio station, a recreation room, and everything else we could think of. They'd had Valentine's Day dances and Christmas parties and the best-haunted houses. What a school! I had been so lucky to have my son there, and I realized it was the best decision I'd ever made for him. Even though he was handicapped, he'd still had a life full of fun. He'd made new friends and learned a lot. It had definitely been the best decision for Kyle. It had given him a life that a regular school system could not have provided.

With so much going on at home, my relationship with Lenny came to an end. I just couldn't continue it any longer. There were some things

I just couldn't handle or accept. Even though I loved him, it was over. Life would be different once again, and I just hoped he could find happiness and peace within himself. The girls kept busy with school and cheering and having friends over at the house all the time. My life was full and very busy.

Kyle's senior year came and went by so fast., before I knew, it was graduation day. We arrived at Mass Hospital School for Kyle's big day, and my family and I looked around anxiously for Kyle. We found him in his cap and gown, driving his wheelchair down the hall, excited to show us his Dynavox speech device. It had come in, and he was using it. He even had a speech ready for graduation. As we went to take our seats, all the students came to the auditorium in wheelchairs or walking, wishing their classmates well and saying good-bye. Watching the students, my eyes filled with tears, and I thought about how much I would miss the students and staff. A staff member approached me and said that Kyle had been upset earlier; tearing up because he wished his father was there. I felt the same emptiness that Kyle did, missing his father.

The students came down the aisle in their caps and gowns, and the music was touching. Staff members made speeches, and all the students received several scholarships each. Kyle received one in memory of his father. It was an emotional time for everyone. Kyle used his Dynavox for the first time to say good-bye to a teacher. He made his family so proud. We watched a video slideshow of all the young grads, with beautiful music to go with it. The slideshow showed pictures of Kyle when he first started at MHS. It included nice words that described Kyle, and his father's music played in the background. It was a touching, unbelievable graduation night!

Kyle graduating from the Massachusetts Hospital School, 2009

Kyle with all of his metals and trophies he has earned over the years.

Chapter 34

I am often asked, "How did you ever survive such a tragic accident?" All I can say is that a person has to have faith, hope, and courage.

Faith is so important. When something goes wrong in life, we need something to believe in. I often prayed to Jesus for comfort, strength, the will to be strong, and the ability to make correct medical decisions, especially for my son. It was the scariest time of my life. I was just like everyone else. I was young, happily married, and raising my three children. I never thought that such a tragedy could happen to my family, especially when my own family didn't drink and drive. Going around the corner on Route 20 that night, our lives were changed forever.

I am so glad I believed in Jesus. My belief gave me hope as I tried to overcome the obstacles before me. I put everything into God's hands. People have asked me, "Don't you blame Jesus for this?" My answer is, "Absolutely not! Jesus doesn't make bad things happen. He is there to help us, and he brings us hope and comfort when needed." Believe me: I felt his comfort—and Mike's guidance as well.

Everyone needs hope. I wouldn't let myself think that I couldn't do what I had to do. I had no choice. This was the road I had to go down, and I had to go down it with my head high, hoping that the end wasn't too far away. Of course, I asked several times, "Why me?" To this day, I have no answer. If I hadn't had hope, I would never have survived. I would have lost control of my children and myself. I couldn't allow myself to get depressed. I had to stay strong, even though, at times, I was dying inside. There were many times when I cried, especially at night.

I couldn't mourn the loss of Mike the way I would have if he'd died of an illness. It happened so fast, and with my whole family so injured, I was numb for the longest time. I lived in the hospitals for a long time, so I couldn't even be in my own home and bed. Even my home turned into a hospital. I knew Mike was gone, but to this day he has always been close to me in my heart. I think of Mike every day, and I will always mourn his loss. I have learned to go on in life and to adjust to all the changes, but I will never forget.

Life is not fair, but we have to make the best of it. We are our children's role models. They watch how we handle all matters of life. If I had been without hope and had been negative all the time, I would have showed my kids the wrong way to handle life situations. I would have lost each of them, and they wouldn't be where they are today; strong, responsible individuals, who can take control whenever they need to.

You need courage to be strong and to speak up when necessary. We should not be afraid to ask questions and follow our gut feelings. We need courage to raise children who are happy, confident, secure, independent individuals. We need determination to go after what we and our families need. We can't worry about what others say. We must have the courage to do what is right for ourselves as individuals. What is right for one person may not be right for another. Everyone is different. Have the courage to grieve and cry, but know that you need to overcome the situation by being strong and moving forward. There is no time frame for grieving. I still grieve today. But we must have the courage to accept what has happened; knowing that we can't change things or bring back what was has been taken from us. Life goes on, and life is for the living. We have to love ourselves and be happy as individuals before we can love others and make them happy. We need the courage to say, "I can do anything I need to do." There should be no *can't* in our vocabulary.

After losing someone so young and special, I wondered why he had died instead of me. I went through survivor's guilt. There was no answer, but I chose to focus on the happiness he brought into my life rather than the short time I'd had with him. Those short nine years with Mike were the happiest years of my life. I experienced a healthy and loving relationship, and true love. So many people never experience it, but I was blessed with a good man. Having the courage to accept what had been taken from me was difficult. Faith helps to give us hope and the courage we need to survive.

One thing for sure, a mother's love is unconditional. It is something that can't be bought. It is a real love like no other. I had to love my son enough to tell him it was okay if he wanted to be with his daddy, but that if he stayed here with me, I would love him and be with him every step of the way. Jesus and Mike sent Kyle back to me, and I felt so thankful. I knew Kyle had a purpose here on earth. I stayed by Kyle's bedside for many months, which then turned into years. Kyle has taught his family many things—most importantly to appreciate what we have. I always say, "Don't focus on what we don't have; focus on what we *do* have." We must cherish our memories and let them bring laughter, not sadness. We must try not to focus on pain or on the things that are going wrong with us. We must think positively, believing that there is a solution to each problem.

I'm often asked, "Do you forgive the man who killed your husband and paralyzed your son?" I answer, "How do you forgive a man who blames his behavior on ADD?" In his apology letter, Keith never mentioned using cocaine, but he admitted to drinking alcohol and driving recklessly. Truthfully, I try not to give him much thought. I know it won't change the events that took place back on that dreadful night. Thinking about Keith won't change the fact that my husband is gone and my son is paralyzed. I need to focus on what is happening today. My children and I have to survive this; so focusing on Keith wouldn't get me very far. Knowing that he was put away helped a lot. I know it won't be long before he will be a free man, and then I'll worry that he will hurt someone else. It's not about my family anymore. It's about society and everyone staying safe.

I had to accept help from people I didn't know, people who brought my family members and me back and forth from Spaulding Rehab in Boston for many months. Family and friends watched my girls, even when my daughters were having very hard times emotionally—acting out, being mean or bossy, and trying to adjust to their lives being flipped upside-down. I had to learn to trust people and to realize that it was okay that things were not being done the way I would do them. The situation was temporary. I was especially reliant on my family. I could never have survived this ordeal if they hadn't been there helping me. I had to be able to put myself where I was needed most, and for me, that meant being with Kyle, as he was in critical condition for a long time. It was very difficult, but whenever I had free time at home, I tried to make it special with the girls.

People need to grieve and find what works for them. When I was able to be home, I visited the cemetery often. I sat with Mike for a long time, just telling him all my problems. Sometimes I went for walks, and when I was angry and crying hysterically that my life was so hard, I even threw rocks at trees. I missed Mike so much and thought about all the pain Kyle was in. I was helpless. At Spaulding Rehab, I always talked to people. I didn't care if it was a stranger, a nurse, or anybody who would listen. It helped. I had to talk about Mike, because I was missing him so much.

I remember sitting with Kyle one day, when a doctor came in to see how I was doing. I was surprised, as everyone's concern was always for Kyle. She asked me if I was sleeping, and how I was handling everything. I said that I slept when Kyle allowed me to, and I talked a lot to everyone, which seemed to help. She thought that was good. She came by every couple weeks to say hi, and we became friendly. I loved her visits. We talked about Mike a lot, and I will never forget one thing she told me. She said, "It seems like both of you were very happy and were in love with each other. People who don't have regrets in their relationship seem to grieve better, because they know they were good to each other. People who have lots of regrets just can't seem to move on." This made so much sense to me, and it always stayed with me, because I didn't have any regrets. I was very much in love with Michael, and there was nothing I wouldn't have done for him. I had been a good wife, and I knew I'd made him happy.

One of the biggest things for us to remember is that life does go on, and we have to make the best of it. One of the promises I made to Kyle was that I was going to give him a fun life. We would still do things together but in a different way. We had so many challenges, but we still had fun between his surgeries. Kyle was always willing to try anything. One winter we put him on a huge sleigh used for hunting. We made it like a bed, and his friend Dan held him up on it. Lenny hooked the sleigh to his snowmobile and gave Kyle a ride. He loved it!

Kyle even went tubing. He was with his sisters, and Lenny was pulling them behind a jet ski. Somehow the tube tipped over, and everyone was looking for Kyle. Lenny found him under the tube, facedown in the water! That was scary, but Kyle was okay. He got over it quickly and was ready for the next adventure.

That is one great thing about Kyle. Just because he is handicapped doesn't mean he'll let himself stop living. He has been to Las Vegas and Disney World three times, even going on the roller coasters, and he has gone down the slides at water parks. My boyfriend Earl and I take Kyle out every weekend to his favorite Chinese restaurant, the Kahula, and then we're off to Lazo's Cafe. He loves it! He meets up with so many people he knows and is always making new friends, especially with the ladies. Kyle loves going on a pontoon boat, with family and friends. The water is great therapy for him and he is enjoying some fishing.

There are times when Kyle is so tense that I'll ask him what's wrong. He says, "I am so excited! I always have so much excitement in my life." That is when I realize that my daughters, all Kyle's wonderful Personal Care Attendant's, family, friends and myself have done a wonderful job in keeping him happy.

Chapter 35

I learned a few things about traumatic brain injuries and comas. I know that every situation is different, but here are some facts to keep in mind.

1. When a person is in a coma and has a traumatic brain injury, don't forget about muscle tone. Look at the patient's feet. Putting on a cast might be helpful in breaking that muscle tone.
2. Always follow your gut and believe in yourself. I know that my gut feelings were correct several times.
3. Always look at your loved one's eyes. I could tell that something was wrong with Kyle because of his eye color, and then we found out that he had a liver problem.
4. Even though your loved one is in a coma, don't be afraid to talk or read to them. I had always been told that my son wouldn't know who I was and couldn't hear me. But I always knew that Kyle felt my presence. He would squeeze my hand, or the monitors would go off when I spoke. This happened especially when his father's music CD was finished playing. Doctors thought it was just a coincidence, but I felt that it wasn't.
5. A mother knows her child, and she will find a way to do whatever needs to be done. Don't ever give up. Stay positive. Don't ever be afraid to give your opinion on a matter. Whether it is in a school or hospital environment, your opinion and thoughts do matter.

6. Always remember that when a person acts out at times, it doesn't necessarily mean he needs medicine. It could be a response to the people he is working with. Maybe someone is not a good match for your child. You are your child's best advocate, and no one knows him better than you.

7. Always listen to your child carefully. You need to be able to read through the lines.

8. Spastic dystonia (muscle tone) can travel to a new location when you fix one part of the body. If your loved one has severe dystonia, I encourage you to look into a Baclofen pump. It has been a lifesaver for my son. It may not take away all the muscle tone, but it definitely helps with spasms.

9. I regret not keeping Kyle's body jacket on him after his spinal fusion. The jacket prevented him to a certain point from leaning to the right. He lost three inches or more within the first year when we took the jacket off of him. In most cases it's not necessary, Kyle's dystonia was so severe that it should have stayed on. We had no way of knowing what his muscle tone would do. Kyle's brain injury was so severe, and his muscle tone just kept traveling through out his body.

10. Botox works really well. It's temporary, but it helps to relax the muscles.

11. Never give up hope. Have faith. Maintain the courage you need to survive whatever path you may go down. You can do this, especially if you have love! Stay focused and always think positively. Focus on what you do have in life. Just because your life is different doesn't mean that your life is over. You will find ways of doing things and new things to do. Life is always full of adjustments. Don't ever give up! If there is a will, there is a way!

12. Check out your health insurance to see if you qualify for Mass health insurance or your State health insurance. Regular insurance does not cover all medical needs. Since Kyle is disabled, it became a secondary insurance and a lifesaver.

13. Never give up hope. Always have faith. Have the courage to accept what has been given to you, and always remember that you can do this! We choose how we think. Choose to think positively, not negatively.

Health insurance has been a problem for Kyle and me since day one. Our regular insurance didn't cover all of Kyle's medical expenses, and I was instructed to apply for Mass Health immediately after our accident, because Kyle had been disabled. Mass Health was a blessing for us, as it covered all the medical expenses from all three hospitals, all the therapies, and Kyle's wheelchairs. Wheelchairs range in price from $25,000 to $30,000 for a motorized chair and $10,000 to $15,000 for a manual wheelchair. Bath chairs and slings were also covered. Diapers and medicines required low co-payments.

Mass Health did not cover barrier Free Lifts and a handicap vehicle. Mass Health would give us a Hoyer lift, but with my being disabled, I couldn't do the cranking or move the device around. Without the Barrier Free Lift, it would have been hard to take care of Kyle. We used it to get him out of bed and into his chair, out of his chair into bed, and from bed to taking a shower. This lift has a track in the ceiling, and with the push of a button, a strap comes down. We hooked Kyle's sling up to it, pressed the button, and up he went.

We are very fortunate to have Mass Health, and I am so grateful. All of Kyle's twenty-five surgeries and all his doctor's appointments and day procedures are fully covered. All foot braces, body jackets, neck braces, headrest extensions, and casts have been paid for. Kyle was able to attend a special school for his needs, which was a huge blessing to us.

This accident has caused Mass Health millions of dollars, but Keith, the man who hit us, isn't obligated to pay anything. I wish there was a law to rectify this. I don't think it's fair that someone who causes an accident like this doesn't have to be responsible for medical costs. I wish there was a law requiring that a person who gets out of prison have a certain percentage taken out of his income to pay back the state.

My family's medical bills were so high that our insurance put liens on us. I called Attorney Anthony Salerno, he was able to have the liens dropped, and also handled our auto accident case. Mr. Salerno was a blessing to our family, he knew I had so much ahead of me with raising my two little girls, a handicap son, and myself being disabled that he chose not to be compensated. Through the years I was able to provide so much more for my children because of his generosity.

Social Security has been a huge blessing to us also. I was able to collect Social Security for my three children under Mike's Social Security. The only law that needs to be amended, in my opinion, is the one that says that a child can no longer receive Social Security benefits when he reaches eighteen or is finished with high school. A parent who has been divorced has to pay child support until the child has finished college. Why is a parent obligated to pay support but the State isn't? It seems to me that the parent is being punished for getting divorced. It was even worse in our case, because it involved a death, and myself disabled, and there was no way of getting any further support.

Chapter 36

My girls have grown into beautiful young ladies, so mature and responsible. Both have graduated from high school and are currently in college.

Kimberly attends Rhode Island College and is majoring in nursing. She has two more years of college and would love to work in the neonatal unit.

Katie, a student at Worcester State University, is majoring in biology. Her goal is to be a physician's assistant and work at Children's Hospital in Boston. She has five years of college remaining.

Both girls have been on the dean's list and are doing great. I couldn't be prouder of them. They have been involved in the medical field since they were three and five years of age. They have helped me with their brother, Kyle, since the accident happened. I taught them to change bandages, take care of bedsores and incision wounds, and even handle IVs. They helped with Kyle's bathing, hygiene, dressing, rolling and turning him in bed, positioning, and putting on AFOs, body jackets, stretching exercise and hand splints. My daughters took part in all of Kyle's care. They are both very nurturing young women and I have been blessed to have them.

This tragedy has definitely made our family stronger and closer. We all try to make Kyle's life as adventurous as possible. Giving him things to look forward to is the key to keeping him happy. When my girls came home from school—and now college—the first thing they did was to put their stuff down, find their brother, give him a kiss, see how his day had been, and share their day with him. It's a priceless, loving relationship they have with their brother.

Both girls are doing great overall. I couldn't be prouder. They are not just beautiful on the outside but on the inside also. Kimberly and Katie are very giving, loving girls, who are very sensitive to people's needs and wants. I know these qualities will make them thrive in the medical field and in their personal lives.

Kyle has gone through several more surgeries—twenty-five to be exact—and it's been sixteen years since the accident. Kyle started his new day program at the Center of Hope and is doing well. He has adjusted, loves his one-to-one, Ben, and is making friends. Our transition went very smoothly, and everyone at the center was helpful in any way they could be. We still take Kyle to Mass Hospital School to visit, and he loves to see the staff and his friends. Kyle started having seizures three years ago, but he is doing well. He takes nine pills a day, just for seizures.

He is a very happy and content young man, full of laughter and fun. He loves to go out on weekends. He meets up with friends no matter where he goes, and he is still hoping a girl will just hold his hand and spend time with him. Kyle always manages to get the attention of the prettiest girls using his iPad with a speech program. He is not shy at all, and he is a very determined young man.

I think back to when he was in his coma and the doctors had no hope for his survival or that he would be any more than a vegetable. How lucky we are to have come to where we are today. It's a miracle, and one that I am so thankful for. I would be lost without him. Kyle is such an inspiration to so many people and especially to his sisters and family. Everyone knows not to complain to him. Their problems can't even compare to what he has gone through. When they do complain, Kyle always says, "It's a piece of cake. Suck it up, and you will be fine—or try being me for a day and see how it is." That always works. We always hear people say; "I guess I don't have it bad after all. Kyle's the wrong person to complain to!"

Kyle's new adventure is his participation in 5K or 10K races with Mike DiDonato, a man I met in a bike shop. Kyle races in a special running chair that Mike made for him. Mike pushes him in the race, acting as Kyle's legs and arms. It figures that his name is Mike. We felt like it was a sign of good things to come.

Kyle and Mike have been running together for three years now, and they call themselves Team Unstoppable. Their motto is: "Never stop dreaming." Kyle wanted the name Team Unstoppable, because he had played sports his whole life, and he felt that, having survived his coma and recovery, he was unstoppable. He had been determined, motivated, and strong in overcoming his tragedy. The phrase "Never stop dreaming" refers to his continuing dream of playing a sport again, and now Mike has given him a sport that he can be part of. Dreaming is good, and dreams can come true!

This summer Kyle and Mike started doing triathlons, and they are swimming and running together. We are currently working on a bike, hoping that next summer they will be biking together. In this sport, Kyle is the captain and Mike is the angel. Kyle feels like he has a sport again, and we are so thankful for Mike and for all the time and energy that he puts into this. Mike and Kyle have formed a beautiful relationship and a special bond with each other. After each event, Mike kisses Kyle good-bye and tells him he loves him. For more information on these special running chairs, you can contact Mike DiDonato at Mike.didonato@ Southbridgetool.com. Or Team Unstoppable on Facebook.

As for me, I am in a good place. I have come far. Life has thrown me some sharp curve balls, but I am determined to hit a home run. I won't let anything get in the way of my raising my children and making them thrive in life. I live with a lot of pain in my left arm, neck, upper and lower back, and my left side, and I have spasms in my legs. I try to ignore the pain and make the best of it. At this point, I have had four surgeries, but I feel content and happy otherwise. I don't focus on the pain. Instead, I try to focus on my children and keeping them happy. It has worked so far, and I hope and pray that God will continue to give me the strength and courage I need to get through life's obstacles.

I have a good man in my life. His name is Earl, and he treats me like a princess. He is really good with my children, and especially Kyle. He has been a blessing to all of us. I still talk to Mike often, as he will never leave me. He is my strength, and I feel that we have done a great job of raising our children together. I have always followed our mutual values and beliefs and have instilled them in our children to raise them properly. I will keep Mike in my heart always, and someday when we have grandchildren, I will make sure they know what a wonderful man their grandfather was.

Even after sixteen years, I still have days when I instantly come to tears while thinking of Mike. I often wonder where our life together would have taken us and what we would have been doing. I also wonder what Kyle would have done for a career. Would he have gone to college or trade school? Would he have married? Would I be a grandmother? I guess I will never know, but I am so thankful that I had Mike in my life and that I still have my handsome son. I am definitely blessed.

I feel like the past sixteen years have taken us through a series of obstacle courses, but we've gotten through each one of them so far. Soon Keith, the man who hit us, will come up for parole, which will mean one more trip to court with my family. We seem to go to court every two to three years. Hopefully, we never have to lay eyes on him again. My only hope for him is that he can find peace within himself after realizing what he has done. I hope he will see that he can't blame ADD for his actions. He made the wrong choices, drove while intoxicated, and used cocaine. He will be a free man soon, and I hope that the registry will consider his record of speeding and violations and will keep in mind that he killed a wonderful, caring husband, father, son, brother, and uncle at the young age of thirty-nine. I hope they will also consider that he disabled a young boy at the age of ten, taking away many positive aspects of his life and giving him a life of pain and suffering.

All we can do is pray that the registry will never give Keith a license again, that they will keep him off the road and prevent him from hurting anyone else. We need to keep our roads safe. The victims of drunk drivers suffer horrible pain, and I wouldn't wish it on anyone.

Our lives have gone down a long and curvy road, just like the one where our accident took place on Route 20. Now I pray and hope for a smooth road in the coming years.

*Kyle, the Captain, and
Mike, the Angel, competing
in the running portion of
their first triathlon, 2013.*

*Team Unstoppable, Kyle
and Mike, before the
water portion of their
first triathlon, 2013.*

*Mike carrying Kyle
after the swimming
portion of the race
to his running chair
in a triathlon they
competed in, 2013*

Our family, Kyle, Kimberly, Lisa (mother), and Katie.

Kyle and his four sisters, from left to right: Katie, Kimberly, Cassandra, and Breanna.

About the Author

Lisa Brodeur was born and raised in Southbridge, Massachusetts, by her parents. She is the youngest of eight children and has two brothers and five sisters. Lisa is currently living in Charlton, Massachusetts, with her significant other, Earl; her two daughters, Kimberly and Katie; and her son, Kyle.

Lisa's book, her memoir's of being struck by a drunk driver, who also had cocaine in his system, struck her family's car on the evening of November 1, 1997, the driver forever changed her family's lives. Lisa is disabled from the accident and takes care of her son who is paralyzed.

To contact Lisa, e-mail her at Lisaabrod@charter.net.